TO BIND UP THE BROKEN HEARTED

A Foundation in Christian Counselling

Elizabeth,
found this is (did buy it despite evidence
to the contrey!!) thought it might be
useful?! Allyy/x

TO BIND UP THE BROKEN HEARTED

A FOUNDATION IN CHRISTIAN COUNSELLING

MIKE SHELDON AND DAVE AMES

Mission to Marriage

Bible quotes are from the
New International Verson © International Bible Socity
1973, 1978, 1984

Front and back covers by **Cambridge Pre Press**

British Library Cataloguing in Publication Data
Sheldon, Mike
To Bind Up The Brokenhearted
Psychology - Christian perspective
Title II. Ames, Dave
ISBN 1-898859-02-7
Printed in Great Britain for

Mission to Marriage

by
Indeprint
6-7 Leapale Road, Guildford GU1 4JX

DEDICATED TO:

Our wives who were a constant source of encouragement in our own personal frustration as schedules seemed to make the whole project impossible.

And

Those committed people all over the country concerned that truly Christian counselling be made available to every believer and have done something about it!

ACKNOWLEDGEMENTS

As Christians considering counselling many of us will have a tendency to look on it somewhat as a continuum with Sigmund Freud on one end and Jay Adams on the other. Although we and our close colleagues have found our niche somewhere in between, we acknowledge a debt of gratitude to those who have searched for answers and taken the trouble to record and share their findings. If they provided no other service they at least formulated ideas that could be examined in the light of science, common sense and the authority of the Scripture. Even if sometimes they failed to show us the way, they have at least shown us the way not to go.

TO BIND UP THE BROKEN HEARTED

CONTENTS

FOREWORD

BY DR MERVIN SUFFIELD

Over the last 15 years, we have seen a monumental growth in the interest and practice of Christian counselling. Church leaders, who had previously poured scorn on counselling, are now embracing it and sending their people on training courses.

For many, Christian counselling has been life-transforming. Many general medical practices which offer counselling have seen a 50% reduction in referrals to psychiatric services. Churches which have previously seen life problems as either demonic or moral are now viewing them less black or white and are adopting a more caring attitude.

A decade or so ago, many of us involved with counselling through our professional practices were concerned about standards, competence and training. At the time, the only real body to accredit counsellors was the British Association of Counsellors (BAC). In 1993, the Association of Christian Counsellors (ACC) was formed, creating a mechanism which has vastly improved the standard of training and produced an accrediting process recognised nationally. With a good deal of the training ideas and concepts coming from America, many Church leaders and theologians were concerned about the integration of humanistic counselling models into Christian teaching which has inevitably led to many questions.

This book is the best I have read to date. It is well thought through and comes from a clear biblical basis. The authors have not been afraid to tackle many of the difficult areas which have arisen in counselling. Both Mike Sheldon and Dave Ames, write and speak from a wealth of research and personal experience in biblical counselling and training of Christian counsellors and they have not 'pulled any punches'. This book has been approached with a biblical view of humanity without ignoring the many insights from different models of counselling. It provides a framework of scriptural logic enabling us to discern which practices can be used and which are in danger of compromising biblical authority.   Although this book has been written to biblically-based counsellors, it would be equally helpful for Church leaders and others interested in becoming more effective 'people helpers'. It has been written with many different cultural and professional settings in mind which gives it a unique position. This book is not only an enlightening read but would serve well as a text book for counsellor training.

Mervin Suffield

INTRODUCTION

DAVE AMES' BIT

Mike Sheldon was in charge of the counsellor training programme for YWAM when I first met him. We were both delegates the to a committee that eventually formed the Association of Christian Counsellors. I represented the Association of Biblical Counsellors and Mike - YWAM. We sensed a certain kindred mind set although we certainly don't agree on everything. Mike was the chairman of the accreditation committee. (He is the guy to blame for all those long forms and records involved in accreditation.) I was the chairman of the theology committee. (Which was so important that it went out of existence.) Writing this book is Mike's idea. He wanted to write a book to help those who are beginning to feel they could be of greater help to their fellow sojourners if they had the benefit of counselling skill. However, he was concerned that the Christian world view of new counsellors would be expanded in this area at the same time counselling skills are being developed. To this end Mike was looking for a partner in this project and I felt very honoured that with such a plethora of qualified people around he asked me to be his partner.

Writing a book with someone else always presents difficulties even if the coauthor is one's spouse (my experience). For a book to be written by two busy people, operating in two different spheres with enough geographical separation to preclude easy consultation, obviously compounds the difficulties. Some of the difficulty was alleviated through the use of e-mail by allowing us to send complete chapters back and forth to assure we were both speaking with one voice on matters of position, sensitivity and application of Christian principles. Unfortunately, it has taken just over four years to complete what could have well been written in six months in a bit more normal world.

The structure required in a coauthored book generally involves a passive voice and a somewhat impersonal 'we' rather than a much more personal 'I', but there are places where we couldn't speak that way and so we broke the mould by saying 'I (Dave)' or 'I (Mike). We wanted to do this rather than write alternate chapters as personal statements, because the things that are being said have been thoroughly 'argued' through in detail and we are both willing to back every sentence regardless of who originally typed it.

There will always be a dilemma in Christian counselling as mortals seek to integrate the fact of the sovereignty of God with our awareness of some obvious psycho dynamics involved in human problems. On one side some deny that there are any emotional repercussions of past trauma, it is all a matter of rebellion against a sovereign God. At the other extreme therapists view human problems as the natural evolutionary process of a given set of circumstances with no acknowledgement of a God who is in control and working through that particular contexts. We do believe that emotions are very real and that they usually must be acknowledged and reckoned with as a part of any real life change. We also believe that both the emotions and the catalyst that produced them are tools in the hand of God as he conforms us to the image of Jesus. Some words written by Julian of Norwich (1342 - 1416) suggest that concern with godliness may save a lot of psychoanalysis.

> On another day, I was again contemplating what I had been shown about the mixture of affections that troubles our soul in this life.

I saw that it is surely easier and quicker for us to come to a knowledge of God than it is to know our own murky soul, disturbed as it is by rampant affections.

But in the innermost place of our soul, there is God. He is the Creator and foundation of our soul. We are so firmly grounded in God—and so highly treasured by Him—that it is wiser to fix our soul in the knowledge of God first. And then, by comparison with His wisdom and loving intent for us, we can come to know our soul aright.

In the light of God's being we can rightly discern our own motives and correct them.[1]

The idea that she is proposing that seeking God is far less complicated than attempting to string together a series of cause and effect experiences in our 'murky' soul is exactly the thing that can make Christian counselling look simplistic to some. We genuinely have no problem with the use of psychology by committed Christians who accept the Bible as their final authority. Psychology is, at least theoretically, neutral with regard to moral values. Psychotherapeutic techniques take on the values of their authors. Any reference to psychology in this book that seems to be less than favourable is probably referring to the use of psychotherapeutic models which are less than Christian and not merely the usage of psychological observations and techniques which are neutral in value.

There are many books written about counselling, some good and some not so good. Why add another one? When I first met Dave Ames we were both aware of the paucity of books about the Christian approach to counselling, and felt that an introductory text was important to guide people into the counselling literature. Both of us have been involved in developing basic courses in Christian counselling and recognised that an introductory textbook was needed, which did not espouse one approach over any other, but rather enabled the student to understand and thus choose between the myriad voices in the counselling arena. A lot of authors seemed to feel it was their responsibility to either develop a new model or to spell out in detail the failures of all Christian models except for their personal choice of existing models. It has been our aim and purpose to provide the basic values and principles to allow inquirers to make intelligent, informed decisions on their own.

Why write the book together? Certainly it would have been easier to write it alone. When no-one challenges your views it is surprisingly easy to get carried away on the tide of your own opinion. Dave and I are quite different, and so hoped to complement each other. This was a painful, yet fruitful activity, as we both grew to understand the value of another's viewpoint. It has been an interesting time as we attempted to produce a coherent whole out of two very incomplete parts.

We are aware that the one sentiment you will experience frequently when reading this book is frustration. That is because we have only lightly touched upon many subjects which you wanted to be covered in more detail. We have indicated throughout the text that this is a 'milk' book, and that after reading it you will want to get your teeth into some real 'meat'. However, it is important to first feed on milk as any baby will tell you. The term milk is used to indicate basics - foundational material but unfortunately, we know several experienced Christian counsellors who have developed their skills without the benefit of a truly Christian foundation. This is the difference between Christian counselling and a Christian who counsels. We trust that this introduction to the vital area of Christian counselling will whet your appetite and lead you on to a deeper insight into the ways in which we can serve God through the counselling ministry.

END NOTE

1. *I Promise You A Crown*, pg. 116 & 117, arranged by David Hazard, Bethany House

PEOPLE HELPERS

HELP ME!

Imagine that you have just sat down with a cup of hot chocolate after a hard day's work, and your thoughts turn to a good night's rest. The telephone rings and Mary, who is a neighbour of yours, is on the line. She is in floods of tears and says that she is at the end of her tether and can't cope any more. Her husband has left her with their three young children and gone to live with another woman. The children are crying and she doesn't know what to do. She cries: 'Please help me.'

DO TO ONE ANOTHER	
The Bible contains many commands about how we should treat one another. Some of these most relevant to counselling are ... one another	
Encourage	1 Thess. 5:11
Care for	1 Cor. 12:25
Accept	Rom. 15:7
Be kind to	Eph. 4:32
Comfort	2 Cor.1:4
Serve	1 Pet. 4:10
Bear burdens	Gal. 6:2
Forbear	Eph. 4:2
Confess sins to	Jas. 5:16
Forgive	Eph. 4:32
Admonish	Col. 3:16
Build up	Rom. 15:2
Pray for	Jas. 5:16
and above all	
LOVE	Jn. 13:34 (and many others)

What do you do? Do you make some sympathetic noises and put her off? Do you attempt to pass on the problem to someone else? Do you tell her to phone the doctor? Do you groan inwardly and try to pacify her with platitudes? This situation, or situations much like it, occur hundreds of times every day, and many Christians feel helpless in the face of such human need. Mary, first of all, needs someone to listen to her. Next she needs some practical assistance, and later she may well need some extensive counselling support. Will you be able to help?

THE COUNSELLOR

Counselling and psychotherapy are two growth industries in our western society. In many countries today a good counsellor is in great demand. Who else can people turn to when they face life's crises which flood them with emotional pain? *Traditional medical professionals already seem to be overwhelmed with people's needs.* Doctors usually have only a small amount of time to spend with each person. This brevity of opportunity and a mainly biological model of treatment - 'Take these pills twice a day for your depression.'- does not adequately address the person's emotional needs.

Why is counselling often successful? A good counsellor will first of all make the person coming to them feel valued and important when the world makes them feel a failure. The client is given the undivided attention and time of another person who is interested in them as a person. The counsellor will listen to the person. Often this is the first time they have really been heard. A non-threatening sounding board will be offered to people to allow them time and space to consider their life and the options they have. Various approaches may be offered to help change destructive beliefs and habits. No wonder there is such a demand for counselling! In America the psychotherapist has been in vogue for decades.

This book is written for Christians by Christians. We (the authors) both have the strong conviction that counselling is an important ministry of the Church today. We believe that all Christians are called to be counsellors in one form or another. Some to be trained as specialist counsellors, others to become listeners and encouragers, but *all Christians are called to be people helpers*. Helping people should be the motto of all Christians, as we seek to obey the great commandment to love God and love our neighbours. However, not every Christian necessarily shares our conviction about the value of counselling. It may be argued that the Church has given up its role in counselling, and now has little or nothing to say to people in need. Others have asked the questions which challenge our assumptions.

Does the Bible, in fact, point the Christian towards a ministry of helping people in the world with their hurts and problems?

Should we only offer help to those already within our own church walls?

Is the gospel of Jesus relevant to the world today?

If it is relevant, how do we interpret this gospel so that people can understand and receive help?

Is there such an activity as Christian counselling?

We aim to answer these and many other questions in the chapters that follow.

THE HOLY SPIRIT

Towards the end of his ministry Jesus said: *'Anyone who has faith in me will do what I have been doing. He will do even greater things than these, because I am going to the Father. .... I will ask the Father and he will give you another Counsellor to be with you forever - the Spirit of truth ..... you know him, for he lives with you and will be in you.'*[1]

Jesus promises that the Holy Spirit - the Counsellor - will be both with us and within us. In John 14 Jesus said: 'You are in me and I am in you.'[2] The Holy Spirit as the Counsellor is presented by the Bible as an advocate, comforter and helper who stands by us, supports us, teaches us the truth, gives us power and assists us at all times. Early in his ministry Jesus had talked about this promised Holy Spirit.[3] Jesus then quotes the prophet Isaiah to explain the work he came to do - to heal the sick, bring good news, bind up the brokenhearted, to set free those in captivity, to release people from darkness, to comfort those who mourn and replace despair with praise. The Holy Spirit is sent to Jesus following his baptism.[4] Then Jesus sends out his disciples to preach the Good News and heal the sick.[5]

Later Jesus promised His disciples that this Counsellor would come and would be in all who believe in him.[6] We know that this happened to the early Church at Pentecost.[7] The Holy Spirit is the Counsellor, and he resides in us to help us mature and become like Jesus so that we may in turn reach out to others in need. This *process* of achieving wholeness and salvation, or growing to be like Jesus, therefore involves *the* Counsellor. So, at the outset, we recognise that Christian counselling is an activity of God through the Holy Spirit. But we will stress that the Holy Spirit usually works through people, using willing believers as helpers and co-workers. *Perhaps we should be called assistant counsellors.*

PEOPLE HELPERS

All Christians are called to be people helpers as we become aware of the needs of our brothers and sisters in Christ and also of our non-Christian neighbours. The Bible has much to say about what we must do for one another. Above all else we must love and serve other people in order to love and serve God (see especially 1 John 3). The response in the secular world to the growing needs of people has been to increase the levels of medical, social and psychological help. One of the main applications of the growth of psychological knowledge has been counselling. But what has been the response in the Church to the growth in need? We would expect there to be a great increase in the ministry of pastoral care. One of the last things Jesus told Peter was to look after His sheep.[8] Then as the body of the Church becomes healthier, the expectation of Jesus (as described in the story of the sheep and the goats) was that Christians would reach out into the community to shelter, comfort and bring hope to those hurting there.[9] But apart from a few exceptions, this doesn't seem to be the model followed by many people within the Church today. The church hasn't always responded to the growing needs as it should have done.

However, a fresh approach has been stirring in some churches. God's heart for the hurting has been responded too and a growing number of people have been seeking to demonstrate the love of God to a hurting world through counselling, prayer and practical helps. We hope that this book will help the church value and develop people helpers.

Many people have discovered that they have a heart to help others, and so turn towards their neighbour. Sometimes this has been recognised as important and the Church together takes on a pastoral and counselling ministry. But at other times such people feel that they have to struggle against a tidal wave of apathy.

God loves everyone equally, but many hurting people are not experiencing that love. We are called to love God first and then reach out to love our neighbour in need. This act of love releases needy people to experience and respond to the Holy Spirit in their life.

COUNSELLING AND THE CHURCH

Christianity has always stressed the importance of caring, helping and supporting people when they are in difficulties. Most Christians would agree that, if loving God and loving our neighbours sums up the Christian message, then counselling in some form can

If my neighbour has a barrier against the love of God....

Perhaps God will use me to come in under the dark cloud to deliver his love at ground level.

hardly be avoided. Paul and James both stress the importance of people-helping as a mark of the Christian faith. Paul states we should help the weak and build up our neighbours, pointing to the Scriptures as the primary tool for hope and encouragement.[10] James argues that having faith in God is not enough unless it is translated into deeds.[11] James also teaches the value of confessing our sins to each other and of praying for one another as an essential part of coming into wholeness and healing.[12]

Earlier in the twentieth century much of Western society faced a crisis as people attempted to retain the moral concept of right and wrong, while at the same time rejecting God. This culminated in the 1960's and 1970's with the rejection of the idea of a universally absolute set of moral and ethical values. Situation ethics have become the norm, with each person attempting to define what is right and wrong for himself or herself. From the world's perspective Christianity has lost its moral high ground, because secular society has 'levelled the playing field' by placing each man and woman in the spotlight, and by denying the need for recourse to any gods or spiritual powers. In fact many people (directly or indirectly) looked to the Humanists for moral guidance. Humanists maintain that all the power and strength to be human exists within the person. With no God, and no need for gods, the helping of people in need has largely been handed over to secular professionals such as doctors and psychologists. This has accelerated the process of secularisation of society where the message of the Church is increasingly marginalised. The growth of secular psychology and counselling has centred on the belief that people can survive without recourse to God.

God's created beings have been offered a belief system centred on science, and then persuaded to put their faith in the power of fallen people. Humanistic philosophy has been the driving force for the bulk of this century. Most theories of psychology and counselling are openly humanistic, assuming that the strength within a person is the main element needed for healing and wholeness. Hence secular psychology has played an important role in building a world view containing a model of the human race that excludes a need for divine intervention. Secular models of counselling have sought to develop ways to change attitudes, beliefs and behaviours without recourse to God. Psychology has become increasingly popular as people feel under increasing stress and see it as a science with answers to problems. People need help. Who can they turn to? *It must break God's heart that the Christian community is often the last place that people in a hurting world look to for help and answers.*

The past two decades have seen the dawning of the *Post Modern* era. People have become disillusioned with the promises of science and many clamour for something beyond themselves. An interest in the powers outside the person has awakened an interest in 'spiritual' matters, and the New Age movement has encouraged a potentially dangerous belief that the entire spirit realm awaits passively for our interaction. A growing interest in the occult has been one inevitable result.

Many of us in the Church have allowed ourselves to be duped and misled in two important ways. First, we have been led into believing that the caring professional using humanistic beliefs is of more value than the Christian seeking to bring God's love and mercy into an impaired life. Secondly, we have been duped into believing that leaving God out of the counselling system makes it 'neutral' and therefore 'safe'. The reality is that there is always an underlying philosophy which inspires the methods used and affects the results achieved. Love is replaced by clinical detachment, and non-dependence, and such phrases as 'enabling', and 'discovering the power within you'. We have been on the very edge of self-destruction. Fortunately God has moved many hearts to seek a renewal in the role of the Christian to bring support, sympathy, wisdom, and love into hurting lives through the ministry of counselling in the power of the Holy Spirit.

CHRISTIAN ATTITUDES TO SECULAR COUNSELLING

When faced with this growth of secular counselling and psychological medicine, what should the Christian's response be? Do we condemn all such counselling help because it is based on humanistic principles? Do we wring our hands helplessly and cry out to God in prayer, not knowing what we can do to help? Do we attempt to beat the secular world at its own game and invent our own counselling methods? Do we just continue going to Church on Sundays, grateful that we ourselves are saved, and hoping that the end of the world is near so that the problems will all be solved by Jesus coming again?

We recognise that there is a growing debate within the Church over the value of counselling, and there is an increasing willingness to re-examine the Christian response. But how should we regard secular methods of helping people? First, we believe that *we should be grateful that many dedicated and well intentioned people in secular situations (many of them practising Christians), have sought to help people in distress,* and in many instances have provided help and support which no one else was willing or able to provide.

Secondly, there needs to be a recognition that there is often much that is good in activities which people create. We are born in the image of God and he sheds his grace on all people even when they don't acknowledge him. But this understanding of God's grace must be balanced by the understanding that man is fallen. The concept of original sin is unpopular today, but we must recognise that all people are made in the image of the fallen Adam as well as in the image of God.[13] This fallen, sinful nature implies that the works we create by our own minds and hands, without God's guidance, are also fallen. Virtually all secular models of counselling have been built on a fallen, and therefore incomplete, understanding of humanity. Although there is often considerable truth contained within a given model, that does not mean that we can use it without danger from the fallen values it also contains. It is true that good people, who sensitively pick and choose what their conscience guides them into, can do many good things for others. In fallen humans the conscience seems to be the most God-like part, and many good people practise godly ways without recognising God himself. If the Church itself is doing little or nothing to help those who are hurting, then people will turn to secular sources for help. Later we will discuss the issues surrounding the integration of Christian and secular methods and the difficulties involved.

Our third attitude should perhaps be to have a deep godly sorrow for the fact that we in the Church sometimes give 'people helping' such a low priority. Often we appear to be more concerned with doctrine than people. We obviously have no wish to devalue sound doctrine, but rather seek to emphasise that Jesus has summed up the Christian life in the great commandment - to first love God, and then to love the people around us. Let us determine to hear God about the redevelopment of this ancient ministry of loving people, and to involve many church members in the process. We may wonder what God's view of recent history is. Is he brokenhearted that the Church has laid down its burden of caring? If that is true, then now is the time to pick that burden back up again. It is vital that all of us should be willing to use the power God has given us to build up the body of the church first, and then to go out and demonstrate God's character and power to heal a hurting world.

THE STRESS OF LIFE

The destructive effects of stress are now well documented and more and more people are willing to admit that they are suffering from its effects. We are constantly faced with a pace of change to which most people find it very hard to adapt. Evil seems to multiply, and although there may be as many good people as there ever were, they seem to be keeping their heads down. Traumatic experiences receive extensive media coverage, bringing harrowing pictures into every living room. This multiplies the impact and induces fear and a feeling of impotence. One rape now engenders fear in not just a handful of the friends of the victim, but also in millions of women throughout the land. Atrocities, like Dunblane, engender fear in many parents concerning their children's welfare. This fear may, in turn, result in a stifling protection which inhibits the child's ability to learn how to cope with the world around them.

Is it any wonder that more and more people feel that the stress is too great for them? Add to this the tremendous changes in family life in recent years which means that, for most people, there is a loss of support and advice from older family members living nearby. As a consequence we have witnessed the virtual destruction of the extended family. Sexual promiscuity has led to an increase in abortions and single parenthood. At the same time there has been a large increase in divorce. Suicide seems to be the only way out for an increasing number of young people. Many children now live in broken or incomplete homes, and the role model of parent and a respected authority figure seems to be almost nonexistent. The preoccupation of the majority today is 'self' and 'my rights' as opposed to 'my responsibilities and duties towards others'.

A new society has been created which values success and achievement, encourages competition and sneers at failure. As everyone fails at one time or another, we have a recipe for disaster. We don't need clever prophets to predict that most western countries are heading for very difficult times because of a breakdown of social values. Wars, famines, murders and disasters are ever present on our TV screens. Many people, both Christian and non-Christian, believe that we are living in the last days.

THE NORMAL CHRISTIAN LIFE?

In the West, Christians are marginalised in what is basically a humanistic society. Worldwide we are clearly in a minority, but we are not ignored. A recent article in *Christianity Today* stated: 'Christians are more widely persecuted than believers of any other faith.'[14] When living the Christian life itself becomes stressful, then issues which may not have been faced previously tend to come to the surface. Many young people are now exposed to a level of temptation, lies and wickedness which is frankly shocking to previous generations. Many young people now dabble with drugs, sex and the occult before they have even left school. Those that become Christians bring a lot of baggage with them that is often difficult to unpack. Receiving counselling is not something for a few weak Christians, but rather something most of us need, in varying amounts, according to the hurts and wounds we still have within us.

SALVATION, HEALING AND WHOLENESS

What is salvation? We all understand that we are saved by believing in God through his Son Jesus Christ. This work of salvation, through the grace of God, is the most precious gift that anyone could receive. Most Christians can give testimony either to a specific time when they were converted, or point to a process over time which eventually led to a living faith and belief in God. Some who had the privilege of being born into a godly family will give testimony that, as far as they can remember, they always loved and trusted in Christ.

But the New Testament also speaks of salvation as an on-going process. For example Paul talks of 'those who are being saved'.[15] Peter also urges that we 'crave pure spiritual milk', so that by it (we) may grow up in (our) salvation'.[16] Have we been offering an easy conversion to a brand of Christianity which does not deal adequately with the consequences of past sins? Salvation takes us out of the Kingdom of darkness and into the Kingdom of light, but unfortunately we don't leave all our baggage and dirty clothing behind. Paul talks about the difference between our old and the new natures. He urges us to put off the old self which is being corrupted by its deceitful desires, and instead encourages us to be made new in our hearts and to put on the new self which is created righteous and holy to be like God.[17] This process of growth into Christ-like maturity and wholeness is a lifelong process. The optimal environment for this transition is within a body of believers - the Church.

27

We are called on to support one another and so build one another up.[18]

But what happens when someone gets stuck? There are times when we need a deeper help than that normally present within our everyday relationships. This is where the pastoral help of the body of Christian believers comes into play. Good pastoral care involves the bringing of biblical truth to bear in a loving, and sensitive way. Many sorts of gifts may be involved. There will be a need to ***teach*** the specific applicable truth and then a need for challenging and ***exhortation*** for the person's life to match up to that truth. There will be need for ***prayer*** to help effect any change, and lastly, a need for the loving, encouraging and practical ***support*** while the often painful period of growth is being experienced.

The Bible declares that we are being adopted as sons of God. [19] Parents who have adopted children are aware that there is usually a process of testing when the child learns about the facts of their adoption. The child is legally the child of their new parents, but to the child the experience is usually quite different. There is nearly always a long process during which the child severely tests the parents. Do you really love me, even when I am bad? Will you reject me as I perceive others to have done? Eventually, if the parents genuinely love the child and support him or her through these trials, the experience begins to match up to the reality. Finally the adopted child both believes and acts as the child of the new parents. This picture of adoption seems to mirror many people's experience of the Christian life.

What sort of issues arise during such times, and why can't they be dealt with within the context of normal Church life? Who needs this process of counselling, and who should provide it? We present in this book the sorts of problems which may affect us, and the types of responses which are appropriate. We recognise that some

Christians will emphasise spiritual warfare while others will emphasise the need for on-going teaching and discipling in order for the Holy Spirit to renew fully the heart of the person. In this introductory book we will attempt to outline the spectrum of pastoral and counselling help which Christians need.

THE PASTORAL MINISTRY

God's primary objective for every believer is that we 'be conformed to the image of his Son'.[20] Maturity in Christ should be the personal goal of every believer and the main objective of every Christian ministry, because this is 'making disciples'. It certainly has to be viewed as the core objective of Christian counselling. Within this process of maturing, the ministries of discipling and Christian counselling may be seen as two sides of the same coin. *Discipling may be thought of as preventative counselling and Christian counselling can be considered to be problem-oriented discipleship.*

What sort of help does the average Christian need? Paul uses the powerful picture of the Church acting as a body. Each member is connected through relationships to many others. Each is part of the body and encourages and supports other parts by looking after their interests rather than its own.[21] Many of us come into Christianity as inward-looking, inadequate people. We often want to be left alone to sort out our own problems. Slowly the experience of living in the Church should draw us out into a more open position where sharing our life with others becomes a more natural activity. This then helps to keep us accountable and growing to become more Christ-like.

29

We should not underestimate how difficult this process is. Often when we turn to others for help within the Church, the very people who should be helping us can be the ones who in fact are deepening our wounds. Most of us can give testimony how other Christians have hurt us. This should help us understand the reluctance some have to make themselves sufficiently vulnerable to experience the sort of life which James exhorts the Church to strive for.[22]

Relationships are of great importance in all our lives, because godliness is worked out through relationships. However, this raises an even bigger problem. Most of the time we can just about cope with ourselves. Trying to cope with other people's problems as well can seem insurmountable. There is the paradox that difficult relationships are the main catalyst in our lives for our personal spiritual growth and, at the same time, the source of many of our problems. Our personality begins to develop in childhood, and usually by the time we become Christians, our character and personality are set in a mould which owes more to the world's way of thinking than to God's. We have been influenced by relationships with parents, family and friends as we have become a 'person'. However, the person we have become as an adult is not the one God envisaged, but rather one shaped in a fallen world through sin and evil (as well as by good). The Christian life involves using the power which God puts within us to develop the new man or woman which is to be eternal. It also involves using that power to become more and more like the character of Jesus.

The process of new birth is the start of dealing with this fallen inheritance. This in turn frees us to become 'real people' who are able to cooperate with others in creating a beautiful and harmonious body of believers. At our new birth God places the Holy Spirit within us,[23] and so *gives us the power to change.* This power to change is absent from all other methods of 'people changing' - including <u>all</u> secular psychiatric, and psychological counselling approaches.

Thus, it is through our difficulties and weaknesses that God works on our character to perfect us.[24] On this path we all at times stumble. We should beware of becoming arrogant in our Christian walk, especially as we become more mature. We should remember that God opposes the proud.[25] He is with us, not to make our path easy and comfortable, but rather to help us grow and mature as we share in the sufferings of Christ.[26] This is a painful process, and we need a lot of help to make the best of the opportunities which this life presents.

SUMMARY

To summarise the main points in this chapter -

1. The traditional, medical professional is already overwhelmed with people's needs, most of which are not physical in origin. The role of counselling is becoming more recognised and Christians must help to fill this void or run the danger of becoming marginalised. Christian counselling could be one of the Church's most efficient discipleship tools and also the most effective method of outreach to the world.

2. Not every Christian is called to be a counsellor, but all of us are called to be *people helpers*. Despite what the church teaches the Christian community is, ironically, often the last place a hurting world believes it can turn to.

3. Unfortunately, large segments of the Church have believed that caring professionals using humanistic techniques are likely

to be more effective than Christians offering counselling. And many Christians involved in counselling have seen models that exclude God as being 'neutral' and therefore 'safe'.

4. Christian counselling differs from secular counselling in both its agenda and its values. For example in addition to aiding the client to take responsibility for his or her life, Christian counselling:

> helps Christians to maturity in Christ
> views the commands of God as the pathway to maturity
> has the answer for guilt
> operates in the power of the Holy Spirit to change

No secular counselling, psychotherapeutic or psychiatric model touches these four important areas.

5. The Holy Spirit is actually *the* Counsellor. To be effectively used by God it pays to view ourselves as **assistant counsellors**.

SUGGESTED FURTHER READING

Understanding People by Lawrence Crabb. Published by Marshall Pickering, Basingstoke, England in 1987.

Lawrence Crabb gives fresh insight into the biblical approach to counselling. It is the best book that we know on the subject.

Right Relationships by Tom Marshall. Published by Sovereign World, England in 1989.

The best book we have seen for making clear the basic elements and dynamics of relationships and linking it in with godliness.

Christian Counselling by Gary Collins. Published by Word(UK), England. Several editions have been produced - mine is dated 1987.

This is a "textbook" of Christian counselling. It acts as a guide to most problems which counsellors face. The book has a very practical emphasis, dealing with many difficult areas.

How To Counsel From Scripture by Martin and Deidre Bobgan. Published by Moody Press, Chicago in 1985.

Psychology Through The Eyes Of Faith by David Myers and Malcolm Jeeves. Published by Apollos (Imprint of IVP) Leicester, England in 1991.

The Bible And Counselling by Roger Hurding. Published by Hodder and Stoughton, London in 1992.

Roger seeks to put Christian counselling within the context of the pastoral care of the local church and also explores its potential within the wider community.

CHAPTER END NOTES

[1] John 14:12-17   [2] John 14:20   [3] Luke 4:18-21   [4] Luke 3:21-22
[5] Luke 9:1   [6] John 14:16-17   [7] Acts 2   [8] John 21:16
[9] Matthew 25:31-46   [10] Romans 15:1-4   [11] James 2:14-26   [12] James 5:14-16
[13] Genesis 3   [14] John Hanford, aid to Senator Richard Lugar, in an article by Charles Colson, *Christianity Today*,   4 March 1996
[15] 1 Corinthians 1:18   [16] 1 Peter 2:2   [17] Ephesians 4:20-24
[18] Ephesians 4:11-13 [19] Ephesians 1:5   [20] Romans 8:29
[21] Philippians 2:3-4   [22] James 5:16   [23] 2 Corinthians 1:22
[24] James 1:1-18   [25] James 4:6   [26] 1 Peter 4:12 - 19

DEFINING COUNSELLING

'Counselling' is a word which is easy to use, but which is extremely difficult to define. If you have ten counsellors together in a room then you are likely to get at least ten different definitions. Despite the difficulties involved in defining counselling, we want to start to explain our understanding of what counselling is.

As we pointed out in the previous chapter, counselling, in the secular sense, is an application of psychology which seeks to help people deal with difficulties. The following statement is a typical definition of secular counselling:

> *Counselling is that activity which seeks to help people towards constructive change and growth in any or every aspect of their lives, through a caring relationship and within agreed relational boundaries.*[1]

When adapting this definition to encompass Christian counselling, we would want to broaden its scope to include other related areas of Christian ministry which are closely associated with counselling. Some may prefer to call these activities 'pastoral care' or 'spiritual direction', but the boundary between them is so obscure that it is helpful to see them as a continuum of help.

Effective counselling requires the following elements:

a relationship with a purpose and setting;

counselling skills used by the counsellor;
a model or understanding of how problems arise in people;
a similar model which describes how they can be helped;
a clear boundary for the relationship.

THE COUNSELLING RELATIONSHIP

All counselling activity must take place within a relationship which is appropriate and conducive to achieving the desired aims. In secular counselling, this relationship is usually well defined and demands certain attributes of the counsellor which facilitate that relationship. These attributes would include warmth of personality, a genuineness of character and an acceptance of people as being of worth and value (regardless of whatever they have done or experienced). We will discuss in a later chapter how this relationship is further enhanced when a Christian counselling model is adopted.

COUNSELLING SKILLS

Each model of counselling will stress and make use of slightly different skills, but the generally acknowledged core skills of counselling include the abilities to listen, to bring understanding, to use empathy to encourage and release, and the willingness to stand by people as they go through crises as an objective 'friend'. We will also discuss these, and other skills, in a later chapter.

MODELS OF COUNSELLING

Each theoretical model of counselling comprises a set of assumptions, aims and methods, and will occur in a specific setting. It is useful to ask the following questions about any new model of counselling we encounter in order to discover what the beliefs and practices are based on. We are indebted to Roger Hurding's book *Roots and Shoots* for this outline of counselling models.

WHAT ARE ITS ASSUMPTIONS?

These are the basic beliefs, assumptions and understanding on which the theory is based. Sometimes they are clearly stated, but often they have to be deduced from the model itself. For example, what does this model presuppose about human beings, and their responsibility for actions?

WHAT ARE ITS AIMS?

These are the stated goals of change desirable within the person which the model seeks to achieve. Often these goals are not explicitly stated, but the student needs to ask: 'What is the intended end result of this method of help?' Is, for example, the aim to help people change their behaviour in ways which are compatible with Christian belief and practice?

WHAT ARE ITS METHODS?

These are the combination of theoretical understanding and techniques which are used by the counsellor to achieve the stated aims. The methods are usually the most obvious part of the counselling model, and most textbooks will describe in great detail the methods used. The student should question whether the methods used are consistent with the stated aims. Most methods of counselling are based on good ideas as well as experimental observation. In any method there will be many success stories, but these are less relevant than an open examination of the strengths and weaknesses of the method.

WHAT ARE THE SETTINGS?

These include the context in which the counselling relationship occurs, the 'contract' or agreement between the counsellor and counsellee, and the boundaries of the counselling interaction. The settings thus include aspects such as the belief systems of the counsellor and client, and the agreed areas which will be explored during the sessions.

In addition to the above, Christian counselling will - as we shall be discussing - also have within its structure some elements of spiritual guidance, reconciliation, encouragement and support, healing of the soul and maturing into wholeness. Roger Hurding describes these four strands of pastoral caring and counselling as spiritual direction, pastoral counselling, healing ministries and prophetic counselling. Some of these functions are clearly more pastoral *care* than counselling. We believe that it is helpful to see all ministry as being on a continuum of help which uses different techniques and approaches, but which all have the same purpose of bringing wholeness and maturity into people's lives.

We must be cautious of seeking too rigid a definition of Christian counselling, as it is but one part of the whole range of God's work in our lives. Yet we must also be wary of being too vague or woolly so that it can come to mean whatever people want it to mean. In the following chapters we will define some distinctives of Christian counselling which we trust will embrace that essential group of activities to which all Christians can subscribe.

[1].   *Roots and Shoots, Roger Hurding*

WHAT IS CHRISTIAN COUNSELLING?

After sitting on committees that have been given the task of writing statements of faith and definitions of Christian counselling, we are both aware there are as many ways of defining the ministry of Christian counselling as there are Christian counsellors. And the list of articles that make counselling specifically Christian could fill a book.

We know Christian counselling starts with knowing God who provides us with an authoritative model of mankind. We turn to the Bible to help us understand God and how he has made us; we also learn what can go wrong with our lives, and what we should do when things do go wrong. The Bible is not so much a rule book, as a guide outlining principles for us to relate to our lives. It is interpreted to us by the Holy Spirit, within the context of a body of 'saints' who are genuinely seeking to know and worship God.[1]

We also know that the primary objective of Christian counselling is to facilitate the development of the character of Christ in the client, because we know this is God's objective for every believer (Romans 8:29). Christian counselling is not telling people what to do or think, but rather helping them to find direction in their lives and assisting them to become the men and women God created them to be. The Christian approach to counselling can also be used with nonbelievers, with the main aim being to allow them to know and understand God more closely.

Of all the distinctive aspects of Christian counselling, one of the most important is the fact that it incorporates the power to help people change. This power does not reside solely within the Christian counsellor, nor is it some nebulous force within the universe. Rather, all power comes from God through the Holy Spirit, *the* Counsellor. We are called upon to co-operate with God who will then enable us to effect changes in our lives. There are, of course, other crucial elements that we will be exploring later.

THERE IS ONLY ONE COUNSELLOR

In the Bible only the Holy Spirit is called the Counsellor. We are **the counsellor's assistant** as we are co-workers with God (1 Cor.3:9). As servants of Christ we are entrusted with God's secrets (1 Cor.4:1), we have the mind of Christ (1 Cor.2:16), and are commanded to go and make disciples of all peoples (Matt.28:19) by following the command of Jesus to love others as he has loved us (Jn.15:12).

THE COUNSELLOR

In every Christian counselling relationship there are at least three persons involved. The person seeking help, the counsellor who is seeking to be a channel of help for them, and the Counsellor, the Spirit of Jesus,[2] who is always with us. He is *the* Counsellor and not you or me. We are called not to be the counsellors, but to be the counsellor's assistants - we are called to first be lovers of God, and then to be people helpers.[3]

The Christian helper is someone who befriends and helps people, and through a combination of prayer, common sense, teaching and pastoral concern acts as a channel. Through this channel

God can come and meet people in the person of the Holy Spirit.

Please note, although we have stressed that only the Holy Spirit is the Counsellor and we are his assistants, nevertheless, in order not to depart from common convention and introduce confusion, we will refer to the person who uses counselling to help people as a counsellor. But, we don't want to lose sight of the fact that we are privileged to be working in partnership with the Holy Spirit.

IS THERE A CHRISTIAN STYLE?

What style of counselling did Jesus follow, and what methods does the Holy Spirit use today? The methods used by the Holy Spirit today will be consistent with the objectives of counselling that Jesus used. Jesus comforted, but also challenged. He accepted the person, but exposed the sin. He brought forgiveness to us, and also demanded we forgive each other. He dealt with doubts and wrong thinking by accurately explaining the character and ways of the Father. He encouraged, but also rebuked. He taught by word, by example and then by leaving his disciples to get on with it. Above all else he did only what he saw the Father doing or what the father commanded him.[4] His heart was one of compassion, sensing the Father's heart and moving in tune with it. These are the things we are to do with people in need as the Holy Spirit, the Counsellor, comes and empowers us to reach out. As we do so, we become the channel for the Holy Spirit to reach into and change other people's lives.

Christian counselling is very much a part of the ministry of the Church. We should remind ourselves of the commands of Jesus at the end of his ministry, which echoed his teaching and example. First he pointed out that all authority has been given to him, and that he is always with us. Then he told us to:

> Go
> Make disciples of all nations
> Baptising them
> Teaching them to obey my commands [5]

A disciple is one who is following a master, absorbing an ideology. Obeying commands is an integral part of the process. However, Christian discipleship takes the concept a step further. We are actually to develop the character of Christ. *For those God foreknew he also predestined to be conformed to the likeness of his Son, that he might be the firstborn among many brothers.* [6]

This is where God's heart is - conforming us to the image of his Son. God loves us so much that he wants the very best for us and the best thing he can think of is that we become just like Jesus. That is God's objective for us and if we are going to have a ministry in someone else's life, it must fit in with this overall design. Helping believers develop the character of Christ has to be the overall objective of Christian counselling. Counselling non-believers involves helping them see the wisdom of adopting a Christ-like attitude and, hopefully, of coming closer to Him in relationship.

To make sense of this final command of Jesus, the Great Commission, we must consider carefully just what are the commands of Jesus that we are to go and teach people to obey. Thousands of books have been written about the teaching and commands of Jesus, but the main principles can perhaps be summarised, as Jesus did, in the Great Commandment:

Teacher, which is the greatest commandment in the Law?

41

> *Jesus replied: 'Love the Lord your God with all your heart*
> *and with all your soul and with all your mind.' This is the*
> *first and greatest commandment. And the second is like it:*
> *'Love your neighbour as yourself.' All the Law and the Proph-*
> *ets hang on these two commandments.* [7]

LOVE GOD: In all aspects of our lives we need to find out what pleases the Lord,[8] to know Him, to obey Him and to acknowledge Him as both intimate Father and Holy Lord of all.

LOVE OTHERS: One definition of love is investing my resources in someone else's wellbeing. Loving others is a willingness to lay down my life to be a channel of God's love.

HOW DO WE TEACH PEOPLE?

Many people have a limited view of what teaching involves, based on their own experience of being taught by a restricted range of teaching methods. A lot of people think of teaching as involving predominantly giving information through lectures, notes, and directed reading. Any learning is then assessed formally by an examination. This is a far cry from the world in Jesus' time in which the apprentice (or disciple) approach would have been pictured when Jesus told his disciples to teach others. Most effective learning involves trial and error, as we use knowledge, put things into practice, and have expert support and help as we learn from mistakes. We can only teach others when we have learned from the Master how to apply his truth to our lives.

We teach people to obey the commands of Jesus by being like Jesus. First we need to love them, then to be with them in understanding. Finally, we need to discern and clearly hear God's voice and bring God's truth into any situation. We need to be able to use the truth wisely to challenge and exhort people. This challenging and exhortation should take place within a trusting and loving relationship which leads people towards the light and truth, and so into a closer relationship with God. This is Christian counselling.

DISTINCTIVES OF CHRISTIAN COUNSELLING

We need to outline the distinctive aspects of Christian counselling, recognising that while the foundational beliefs and principles will remain constant, the approaches, emphases and methods of help used will vary according to the experience of the counsellor and the needs of the person seeking help.

We will attempt to describe the major elements of belief which underpin the Christian approach and indicate the framework within which the Christian counsellor will work.

Christian counselling is not an optional alternative to psychotherapy, but rather the way to direct people's response towards the healing power of God. It utilises our knowledge of God and his plan in order to understand people and their problems. It is important that the sequence of *theology, anthropology* and *methodology* be maintained in order to avoid distortion of the facts. A correct and living theology is the vital foundation for any counsellor. From this understanding of God, we develop an understanding of how men and women, created in his image, were intended to work. Then methods and models can be constructed on the understanding that whatever we design will not be perfect, because God often chooses to act in ways beyond our understanding. It is necessary for us continually to press towards understanding God through a closer relationship with Him in order to understand human beings who were created to operate in concert with God.

THEOLOGY

All Christian models of counselling therapy must start with an accurate understanding of God. These primary theological foundations were crystalized by the early Church and exist in the credal statements which the majority of churches have accepted throughout history. It is however, only through on-going study of the Bible and seeking to know the heart and mind of God, that we are able to discover the day-in, day-out, up to the minute, implications of our theology.

ANTHROPOLOGY

A correct theological basis enables us to work out the place of human beings in God's scheme, what their characteristics are, what makes them tick, how things go wrong, and how to put things right. Thus, a Christian model of how people remain healthy, and the things that affect that health, should always be considered before designing methods of counselling.

METHODOLOGY

Our understanding of God, and God's view of people, provides the basic assumptions for a theory of practice upon which we can develop methods for counselling. For example our theology tells us God is concerned to develop the character of Christ in our lives - to be more selfless. Christian anthropology includes the understanding that the human condition is basically selfish. Consequently, our methodology will need to include the possibility of making clients aware of the consequences of their selfishness and the hope God offers in growing through it.

It is of great benefit if, before we become practising counsellors, we first learn the basis of humility. Each one of us will have slightly different approaches and emphases. We may believe in the same God, but our personality and past experience will lead us to stress different aspects of the character and ways of God, so leading to different types of counselling ministry. *There is no one right way of doing Christian counselling.* There are a large variety of healthy, God-given approaches. However, there are also some misguided and unbalanced approaches, and so we trust that after reading this book, you will be better able to discern the underlying beliefs of any approach to counselling and so maintain a godly, biblical and loving approach to people in need.

Without a doubt, we could list a few rather well known 'Christian' approaches that we would avoid. Our reason for not providing such a list is, not so much to avoid controversy, but more because it is such a grey area. The question would quickly be asked: 'Why did you list them and leave those off?' It is more important that counsellors are able to discern for themselves which systems are healthy. A few questions to ask might be:

Are their main distinguishing features supported explicitly by the Bible?

If not, do they have any legitimate claim to biblical support? (Implicit support)

Is there any danger of these methods distorting other clear biblical teachings?

Are people brought closer to God through these techniques, or do they become adherents of a system?

VALUE SYSTEM?

All counselling involves seeking a change in human beliefs and behaviour and is therefore **never devoid of values**. Every school of counselling ever developed (whether secular or Christian) has its foundations rooted in the personal world view of its founding authors. If that world view excludes God then, in our opinion, the author is attempting to arrive at a solution while missing some vital parts of the equation. Most of those people who have developed counselling models deserve credit in that they have *attempted* to avoid superimposing their values onto their counselling model. However, in the belief that neutrality is scientific, most either deny, or imply a denial of, moral and ethical absolutes. From a Christian perspective, denial of right and wrong is hardly neutral or helpful when seeking to assist people sort out the problems they have.

LOVE, MERCY AND COMPASSION

The term 'Christian counselling' often brings to mind such words as love, mercy and compassion. These are facets of God's character which we associate with healing and wholeness. However, there is a sense in which these are *not* Christian distinctives because the professional code of any counselling accreditation body would require exactly the same qualities. Even if the same language is not used, it is certainly implied. *It is the Christian elements, with which secular counselling would not wish to be associated, that are actually the true Christian distinctives.* They give true depth and meaning to words like love, mercy and compassion. It is not easy to go from an understanding that God is love, mercy and compassion, to creating a methodology of counselling which accurately reflects this. These characteristics, along with tenderness, sensitivity and empathy are the vital core of a Christian counselling model, to which needs to be added certain other crucial truths and understandings. *However, we can only develop a methodology to demonstrate God's love, mercy and compassion when we allow the Bible and not society to define these qualities.*

THE CORE PRINCIPLES OF CHRISTIAN COUNSELLING

The core principles of Christian counselling may be used on all clients whatever their prior beliefs, as the basic beliefs and values of the counsellor are not demanded of the client. In practice this counselling may appear similar to most other core elements of secular counselling theories, as the elements of warmth, acceptance, building a caring relationship, listening and helping the client to understand the nature of their problem, are all present.

The major difference is that there is a clear standard of morality, which although not judgmental, is always present to help clients understand what is right and what is wrong. In the counselling of Jesus, he always loved the person and sought to help them, he never condoned their wrong behaviour, but rather gave the way out through the giving and receiving of forgiveness.

Thus a key difference with other counselling models will be the handling of guilt in the client. Sometimes this guilt is false, and the client can be helped to see this, but at other times the guilt will be real because of wrong doing. This guilt cannot be ignored, but can be dealt with through recognising the issues, through repentance, and through the asking for forgiveness and following it through with any necessary restorative action. It is interesting to note the extent to which secular psychology has 'discovered' the giving and requesting of forgiveness as vital to relationships and mental health.

We now list what we see as the main principles which all Christian counselling models will be based on. You may wish to add a few more of your own. We maintain that this list is essential to mark out that which is distinctive about Christian counselling.

GOD EXISTS AND HE HAS SPOKEN. He reveals Himself through the person of his Son Jesus Christ, his written Word and the indwelling Holy Spirit.

THE CHARACTER OF GOD IS LOVE. This most misunderstood concept also embraces justice, perfection, discipline, and mercy.

PEOPLE ARE SPIRITUAL BEINGS. They are created by God, in his image, for a purpose. This purpose is to live in close relationship with God, to grow in the likeness of God and to rule and have dominion over the world. People are, therefore, moral beings, able to discern right from wrong, good and evil.

FALLEN HUMAN NATURE IS ANTITHETICAL TO GOD'S. We have all turned our back on God. Our own selfishness has separated us from Him.

CHRIST DIED TO REDEEM HUMANITY. The incarnation is all about God coming to where people are to redeem us back to the Father's original purpose. Through the cross we have redemption, healing and wholeness.

GOD HAS A PLAN FOR OUR LIVES. He wants to develop in us the character of his Son.

GOD IS SOVEREIGN. He is involved with his creation on a day-to-day basis. He is in control and able to bring his plan to fruition. Nothing can happen without his permission.(cf Romans 9:19ff.)

MORAL ABSOLUTES EXIST. These are implied by God's righteous character, are written in the Bible, and produce freedom through providing safe limits.

GOD HOLDS ALL OF HUMANITY RESPONSIBLE for right behaviour and demands we accept responsibility for our actions when we fail.

TRUE MORAL GUILT IS NOT A SINISTER INFLUENCE, but a catalyst to motivate fallen people to accept responsibility and repent. This in turn leads to forgiveness and to the removal of guilt.

ILLNESS IS PART OF THE FALL. While illness and suffering is an evil outside of God's wishes for us, nevertheless it is a part of this fallen world, and everyone will suffer and eventually die. Our suffering also hurts God, but he frequently allows it to continue as an instrument to fulfil some part of his plan, usually to produce maturity and growth. Jesus encouraged us to pray for healing and frequently heals, but he does so against a backdrop of the fact that healing and wholeness are never completely achieved in this life.

WHAT DOES THE BIBLE SAY ABOUT COUNSELLING?

The concept of counselling and the word *counsel* in its various forms (counselling, counsellor, and counselled), appears in the New International Version of the Bible 55 times. In every case it is associated with the transmission of wisdom. But is that really what we mean when we speak of counselling today? Surely helping people with their problems involves a lot more than giving 'advice'. We don't need to dissect our childhood to know that a certain action is sinful and will cause harm to us and to others. Such sinful actions are self-centred on our part and therefore need to be stopped. It is, however, extremely helpful to be aware of the dynamics that are involved in a certain behaviour. Frequently we find self-discipline easier when we are made aware of the forces we are responding to when we commit certain acts. But when the Bible speaks of counselling it doesn't mention helping someone get in touch with their feelings. Does that mean that what we have come to know as counselling is not the same thing as counselling in the Bible?

Counselling in the Bible has, at its heart, the gaining of insight about the wisdom of God as it applies to the problems we encounter. But as the Holy Spirit is *the* Counsellor, the extra dimension from the New Testament is the power to put that wisdom into effect in our lives. Thus counselling that is biblical is a process of helping the people to:

a) gain insight into their problem, what it is exactly, and how it has arisen;

b) gain insight into God's ways, what God's truth and wisdom is;

c) overcome the emotional and psychological barriers to accepting God's wisdom;

d) apply that wisdom into their lives with love and power.

One could define Christian counselling simply as:

GUIDING BIBLICAL TRUTHS AROUND EMOTIONAL ROADBLOCKS

CIRCLE OF MINISTRY

The different methods used to help someone are really the variety of Christian ministries. Thus it may involve praying with someone, or deliverance, or encouraging them in self-discipline. All of the Christian ministries may be included, but are they counselling? Perhaps not in the strictest sense of the word, but they may be a part of a counselling session. It will help to consider the accompanying figure which shows a 'circle of ministry'. The Holy Spirit is at the centre and gives the power and enabling for all ministry. God may intervene directly into a person's life, without another person as an intermediary. This is less likely than many imagine it to be, because God places a premium on interdependency within the body of believers, and he broadens the circle of blessing as he involves others.

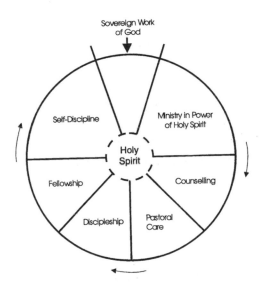

Routinely, we would have counselling where a concentrated period of time is spent with someone where we will help the person discover the nature of the problem and help bring him or her to a biblical understanding of it. We would help the person in the application of that understanding. These sessions may naturally flow on into discipling, and as the person develops a more firm grasp on self-discipline, so the discipling relationship fades into just plain fellowship. Probably most of us have seen such situations through all stages, but realistically the counsellor may have to ask if he or she can afford the protracted investment of time once the counselling stage has closed. Could not someone else be found to take up the discipling stage?

WISDOM

Wisdom is at the heart of counselling in the Bible, but what is the meaning of this word which appears 218 times? An overview of various dictionaries yields a definition like: *combining accurate knowledge with sound judgement to determine appropriate action*. We are told the fear of the LORD is the beginning of wisdom, and knowledge of the Holy One is understanding.[9] The Jews believed that all human knowledge came back to the question of one's commitment to God. So do we! David was delighted with God's framework for living. Psalm 119 consists of 176 statements of how wonderful God's precepts are. But, as already mentioned, counselling is about much more than how we should live - it is also about our difficulty in putting theory for living into practice.

It is interesting that Vine's *Expository Dictionary of New Testament Words* says that the main Greek word translated wisdom, *Sophia* means 'insight into the true nature of things'. That is getting closer to home - like, for instance, 'what is the true nature of my seemingly uncontrollable temper?' Insight and sensitivity are functions of *agape* love. When Jesus commanded us to love one another, did he mean us to simply point out our brothers sin or to search compassionately for insight into the true nature of things so that a given sin pattern might be broken? Counselling is transmitting wisdom, but advice given without understanding *is not wisdom.* 'A word aptly spoken is like apples of gold in settings of silver.'[10] ˑ

Thus, one of the most important attributes for a counsellor is the ability to impart wisdom to his or her clients. What is wisdom and how does one become equipped to be wise and discerning as a counsellor, able to distinguish truth from error? J.I. Packer writes:

> *Wisdom is the power to see, and the inclination to choose, the best and highest goal, together with the surest means of attaining it. Wisdom is, in fact, the practical side of moral goodness. As such, it is found in its fullness only in God.* [11]

The book of Job contains much about suffering and wisdom. Chapter 28 is a poem that searches out this question concerning wisdom. The first two stanzas tell us where wisdom is not found and the third where it is. Job's discussion of where wisdom is not found may well be the more informative to the modern Christian. Speaking of mining precious metals and stones the writer says:

> *Man's hand assaults the flinty rock and lays bare the roots of the mountains. He tunnels through the rock; his eyes see all its treasures. He searches the sources of the rivers and brings hidden things to light.* [12]

Job does not lightly dismiss the technological achievements of his day. He sees them as something to celebrate. To him, they demonstrate how secure man's position is - far above the rest of creation. Job doesn't agree with his 'comforter' Bildad that 'man is but a maggot'. Human beings are not worthless, nor can their triumphs be rejected. But still in verse 12 he asks: 'But where can wisdom be found? Where does understanding dwell?' Going on in verse 13 he asserts: 'Man does not comprehend its worth; it cannot be found in the land of the living.'

Having exhausted Job's offerings as to where wisdom cannot be found, we now have a better foundation to accept Job's answer to his question: 'Where then does wisdom come from?'

God understands the way to it and he alone knows where it dwells. (v 23)

And he said to man, **'The fear of the Lord - that is wisdom.** (v 28)

The subject could be viewed as a continuum, with technology and man's achievements one end, and wisdom the other. This would place modern psychology and philosophy a bit closer to the wisdom end than is mining and technological endeavour. However, we have to recognise that Dr. Packer's definition, 'the power to see, and the inclination to choose, the best', is linked with the concept of *truth* which is an absolute, and such absolutes are not popular today.

Wisdom involves belief in absolutes. These absolutes are not ones which stifle creativity or rule out individuality, but ones which are fulcrums on which individuality and creativity pivot. Technology and science are buttressed by physical absolutes. Wisdom is established on non-physical absolutes, something that most of the secular world will not recognise. We can measure physical absolutes and society can agree on what is acceptable or unacceptable, but only someone outside and greater than society can establish non-physical (or meta-physical) absolutes. We can celebrate the observations which modern psychology has unearthed from the depths of human nature along with many other space age achievements, but these still fall short of wisdom.[13]

THE DIFFERENT SETTINGS OF CHRISTIAN COUNSELLING

Any counselling interaction takes place within a setting or context. This setting has three main elements which we need to understand.

THE BELIEFS AND ATTITUDES OF THE CLIENT

These are of great importance. We often forget that other people are quite different from ourselves in experience, upbringing and beliefs. We must respect the counsellee's own beliefs and seek to understand them. We want to encourage them to emerge during the counselling relationship.

THE BELIEFS AND ATTITUDES OF THE COUNSELLOR

We hope these will always be in line with the mainstream Christian beliefs as outlined above. Note that our beliefs should be tempered with the humility that recognises that none of us has a perfect theology, and a variety of understandings is healthy, as long as the fundamental beliefs are not compromised.

THE RELATIONSHIP WHICH DEVELOPS BETWEEN THE COUNSELLOR AND COUNSELLEE

This will be determined by each person's beliefs, but also by the environment in which the counselling takes place, the boundaries of the relationship as determined by both parties, and the contract made at the start of the counselling, whether written, spoken, or just implicit.

It is important to understand that each counselling setting has *boundaries* which clearly define what sort of interaction should take place within that setting. It is therefore important that clear contracts are made with clients with informed consent and a detailed presentation of the alternatives which could be offered. In the accompanying figure we represent the four main settings in which a Christian counsellor is apt to encounter.

There is always the possibility that settings will change as a case advances. When the setting changes the relationship must be redefined and new boundaries recognised. The illustration serves also as an example of how this might happen. The client is first met in the midst of a crisis, but after four sessions agrees to tackle the main issue in his life. As counselling proceeds he discovers his need for Christ and the counsellor leads him through to Christ. The counselling may then proceed along totally Christian lines and therefore becomes pastoral.

In each of these four settings we will briefly outline the characteristics of each setting, that is: who the clients are; what the basis of the counselling approach is; what the aims of the therapy are, and what the boundaries of the interaction consist of.

1. BRIEF INTERVENTION COUNSELLING   (CRISIS INTERVENTION)

It is important to recognise that there is one aspect of counselling practice which does not necessarily rely on any one theoretical understanding or setting. This method of counselling has been called 'Brief Intervention Counselling' or 'Crisis Intervention'. It may be used in many settings, especially within health care contexts, in dealing with disasters, and in helping people without severe underlying personality problems to cope with the normal problems and difficulties which life brings. It usually consists of a small number of sessions (often not more than six) in which the client is listened to and helped simply to understand their own problems and explore the possible courses of action. Christians can do this as well as any other trained counsellor, as long as the training and experience they have received includes an understanding of the core skills of counselling, and as long as their experience includes counselling with many clients from all religious backgrounds and also from none.

This term is therefore used for a short series of meetings between a client and a counsellor to deal with an immediate problem such as bereavement or acute life stress. A lot of marriage counselling cases are really more akin to crisis intervention than many other types of counselling. If the client needs more help after a few sessions (possibly as many as six) then they need to move on into a more formal counselling relationship in one of the other settings.

The *clients* will be those who present themselves for urgent help with acute life problems, and sex, race, ethnic origin or religious belief has no bearing on the setting. The *basis* of help recognises that the beliefs of the client must be respected and not challenged at this stage. The core skills of a counselling relationship are used to enable the client to have someone to listen to them and support them through a crisis.

Therefore the *aims* are to enable all sorts of people to be helped to discover their problems and begin to explore ways to tackle them. If the problem is straightforward and the client well motivated this may be all the help needed, but often the client will need to be referred on for more specialised counselling help. Thus the *boundaries* dictate that intervention therapy is a transition to either specialised help or healing, either by the original counsellor or a better suited agency. Specific theory of counselling is usually not an issue, but rather the personality of the counsellor building a relationship in which clients are free to explore their problem. The client should usually be referred on for further specific counselling help after a short course of sessions if the issues have not been solved.

2.   *CHRISTIAN COUNSELLING IN THE COMMUNITY*

Christian counselling also has a place within the community, helping those who are willing to accept a Christian approach to their problems. The *clients* are seeking counselling which is based on Christian values and principles, and which will proceed on assumptions about human beings and God as outlined in models of Christian counselling. Many of the clients will be non-believers who have tried other approaches and who wish to see if the Christian approach to their problems will help them.

The *basis* of the counselling is that the client is seeking to know more about themselves and possibly more of God, and they are willing for God's standards to be used, in a general way, in the counselling.   The *aims* are to demonstrate the love of God in action in helping people in need; to demonstrate the power of God in action in changing people and their lives; and so to move people closer to God. There are a great variety of *methods* of counselling help which may be offered. Each of these methods will need to be adapted towards meeting the individual needs of each client. The counsellor will need to be sensitive to the client's beliefs and the Christian aspects of the counselling may not be emphasised at first. Especially we believe that this means that religious language should not be used with non-Christian clients. While biblical truths underpin the counselling, the presentation must be fitted to the experiences of the client.

The *boundaries* are important. If a non-Christian is being counselled and they seek explicitly to know more about the Christian faith, they then step into the salvation counselling setting (it should be made clear that this is happening) and Christian counsellors should avoid putting any sort of pressure on people to make a commitment. It may be best for a person other than the counsellor to help the client if they wish to step into salvation counselling at this stage.

3. 'SALVATION' COUNSELLING (SPIRITUAL DIRECTION)

Strictly speaking, helping a non-Christian to enter the Body of Christ is not counselling but rather spiritual direction. However, the term 'counselling' is widely used within the Church when describing this process of 'leading a person to Jesus', and we should understand the aims and boundaries of it.

The *clients* will be those who acknowledge that they are not Christians, but who wish to know more about God and the Christian faith so that they can make an informed decision. The client has to make an individual decision, but the *basis* of the help given is that the client needs guidance and support to discover the truth.

The *aim* is to help individuals find for themselves the Christian truths outlined in the Bible, and to support them in prayer and with practical help during the time of decision making. The *boundaries* are that the client willingly enters this setting wishing to know about the Christian faith. If the person does make a commitment to the Christian faith then they can pass straight away into a pastoral counselling setting in which problems are dealt with under the Lordship of Jesus Christ.

4.   *CHRISTIAN COUNSELLING IN THE PASTORAL SETTING*

The final setting is that of Christian counselling which is taking place within the context of the Church, (although not necessarily in a church building) where the *clients* would all be Christians who acknowledge the Lordship of Jesus, or those who are back-slidden Christians who wish to be counselled back into a right relationship with God.

The *basis* of the counselling help given will be centred on a model of counselling which acknowledges the importance of God's word through the Bible and through revelation.

The *aims* of this counselling relationship are:

> to restore a right relationship with God;
> to understand more of God's character and ways;
> to restore relationships with others;
> to accept the Biblical view of self as worthy and acceptable in God's sight because of the atonement of Jesus through the cross;
> to develop the spiritual growth and maturity of the client by dealing with spiritual blockages.

The *boundaries* of the relationship require that the person is a committed Christian, who wishes to be counselled according to Christian principles.

BIBLICAL MEDITATION EXERCISE

Take 10 minutes to look up the following references and then meditate on them.

 1 Jn.2:3-6
 1 Jn.4:7-12

 If we love one-another, God lives in us and his love is made complete in us.

We are in danger of forgetting some key tenets regarding the importance of relationships. John says: 'Dear friends, since God so loved us, we also ought to love one another. No one has ever seen God, but if we love one another, God lives in us and his love is made complete in us'. [14] The New Zealand Church leader and author Tom Marshall, whose book on relationships we will be exploring in a later chapter, states that relationships need trust, respect, love and understanding in order to survive.

The ministry of the church to love people involves being involved in a range of activities on a continuum between people helping, which all Christians are called to do as we love and care for those around us, and pastoral counselling which involves some teaching, discipling, deliverance and long term commitment to see people change and then grow to become like Jesus.

CHAPTER END NOTES

1. Romans 15:4   2. John 14:16-17   3. Matthew 28:18-20
4. John 14:31   5. Matthew 28:18-20   6. Romans 8:29
7. Matthew 22:36-40 8. Ephesians 5:10   9. Proverbs 9:10
10. Proverbs 25:11   11. *Knowing God* J.I. Packer, Inter Varsity Press 1973
12. Job 28:9-11   13. We are indebted to Denis D Haack for a good deal
of the ideas on Wisdom, from his news letter *Critique* published several
times a year by the Ransom Fellowship. 1150 West Center Street, Rochester,
MN 55902 e-mail 73653.2770@compuserve.com 14. 1John 4:11-12

SECULAR COUNSELLING AND THE CHRISTIAN

All forms of counselling are growing in popularity and being increasingly accepted as valuable by society in general. The roots of most current models of secular counselling can be traced back around one hundred years ago and owe much of their theory and practice to the early development of psychology.

SECULAR UNDERSTANDING OF COUNSELLING

What does the secular world consider counselling to be? One of the standard

textbooks for counsellor training is *The Theory and Practice of Counselling Psychology* by Richard Nelson-Jones and further development of the ideas and definitions concerning secular counselling which are quoted here may be found in this book. Counselling and psychotherapy are closely linked. Psychology is the study of the mind and psychotherapy is the application of that understanding in helping the person who has a psychological problem. Counselling, as a rule, provides help to less disturbed clients in lay settings whereas psychotherapy tends to help more seriously disturbed people, often within a medical or professional setting. Naturally the boundaries between the two are blurred, and many people refer to 'counselling psychology' in order to encompass the professional activity of counselling.

Counselling, like psychotherapy, aims to help people change their behaviour and use the resources available to them to improve their ability to cope with life. Each counselling model may be considered to have four elements - *basic assumptions and beliefs* which underlie the model; the *theoretical model* itself which seeks to explain how the problems and dysfunction comes about in the person presenting for help; *the aims* of the counsellor who is seeking to restore normal or adequate functioning; and fourthly the *methods and activities* used to achieve those aims and change or modify behaviour.

The theories of secular counselling fall into three main groups - humanistic, psychoanalytical and behavioural. These are in addition to various models based on Christian beliefs.

Because counselling has now spread and developed so widely it is not easy to give a concise definition of all that counselling entails, so this section will outline those elements and activities which are most widely recognised as constituting the activity we call counselling.

COUNSELLING AS A HELPING RELATIONSHIP

The counsellor offers a relationship to the client in which they provide empathy, understanding, respect and genuineness. These are often called the **core conditions of counselling**. They constitute not only the counsellor's skills but also their attitudes of care and concern for the client. The term **active listening** is a way of expressing this basic counselling relationship. Those who view counselling predominantly as a relationship tend to follow the Rogerian, *person-centred* practice of counselling, which is discussed in more detail later.

COUNSELLING AS A SET OF ACTIVITIES

Many counsellors believe that while the relationship between the counsellor and client is important, it is not sufficient on its own to effect the necessary changes. Thus counselling may be viewed also as a set of activities and methods which assist the client to make changes in their personality and behaviour. Here we can see that counselling is indeed a branch of psychology with theories of how to affect these changes in people's behaviour. These are the elements which distinguish between the different models - such as rational-emotive therapy, psycho-analysis and behavioural therapy.

THE COUNSELLOR AS DECISION MAKER

Nelson-Jones in his textbook *The Theory and Practice of Counselling Psychology* stresses that the counsellor is constantly having to make decisions during the counselling process. Counsellors are making decisions about the *role* they have to take in each encounter. 'Does this person need individual attention, or would it be more helpful to involve them in group activity?' Secondly decisions are made of *response*. 'How should I respond to the person's statements and situation?' Finally the counsellor has to make decisions about what *treatment* options should be used.

Counsellors have to make decisions about which particular model or approach to adopt for each client. Many counsellors will describe their approach as *eclectic*, choosing the most appropriate elements from several counselling theories. Some counsellors will stick to one main approach and so develop reasonable expertise in that particular model of counselling, although they may still reject certain aspects of the theory and practice within that model.

THE COUNSELLOR AS AGENT FOR CHANGE

Producing a change in the client is important in all counselling situations. This change may involve the client's beliefs, attitudes, actions and behaviour. The counsellor will normally encourage the client to decide what change is necessary for themselves, then help them to implement that change and later maintain it into the future.

IS COUNSELLING NON-DIRECTIVE?

It is rather naive to think that the beliefs and attitudes of the counsellor have no effect on the counselling process. Even if we say nothing at all we still communicate approval or disapproval through our body language. However hard we try we will all influence the clients we seek to help. We would argue that *there is no such thing as non-directive counselling;* all counselling therapy being directive to a greater or lesser degree according to its theory and aims. It is usually argued that less directive approaches are more helpful for the client, however secular models are based on a relative value system, and Christians will need to re-evaluate this concept in developing their approach. We will consider this in more detail in the next chapter.

CLIENT AUTONOMY

In medical and related work, respecting and maintaining the client's autonomy is a key ethical principle. This means that in the end it is the client who makes decisions about themselves, and the caring professionals are there to advise and help them to make the best decision in their specific circumstances. There is a strong parallel in counselling where to be most effective the client needs to make decisions and make changes in their own life. The counsellor is there to support and facilitate this process. This holds true even in Christian counselling where there is the added dimension of absolute truth in the form of God's wisdom. It is important to realise how we affect other people, and to maintain a sense of humility and sensitivity, allowing other people both to believe and act differently from ourselves.

THEORETICALLY SPEAKING

It is not _absolutely_ necessary to understand secular theory to help hurting people, but it helps. It helps because secular theories were developed to cope in a society that says: 'There is no God'. Therefore secular theories directly address the contemporary mind set helping us to better understand the _Zeitgeist_ or spirit of the age and where many of our clients will be in their thinking. For instance is 'road rage' a disease or a moral issue? We live in what some have termed a 'therapeutic culture' where therapeutic categories displace moral categories to such a degree that moral thinking is completely marginalised, if not politically incorrect. Terms such as health, disease and dysfunction replace terms like responsible and unreliable, wise and foolish. What we often find is the 'pathologising' of sin. We might call sinners 'morally disadvantaged', but such a label would be a contradiction in terms in today's culture.

It also helps to remember that when God is taken out of the picture, we don't believe in nothing, but rather we believe in everything, which could explain why there are so many secular theories. We are not going to drag you through every possibility as there are already entire books dedicated to just that, but we have provided a brief skeleton of some of the most influential. However, we have placed these 20 or so pages at the back of the book as Appendix A. Some people reading a book on Christian counselling would be affronted that we suggest reading even that

much on secular thinking. Others will want to explore the subjects in far greater depth than we can possibly cover. And we
know others who might try reading through the chapter, get bored
and not finish the book. It may well be that your appetite will be
much more whetted to read this material when you have
completed the main text. The appendix was written by Mike and
since it is Dave writing this 'bridge' to it I feel free to say, it
does actually read pretty well - I certainly discovered one or two
new facts!

DON'T MISS IT!

CHRISTIANS AND SECULAR COUNSELLING

There are many people who believe that Christians engaged in counselling may, in addition to a Christian model of counselling, also use secular models of counselling providing it is properly integrated without compromising Christian beliefs and practices. There are also a large number of Christians trained in secular counselling models, who have adapted these models, or who use those parts of the model which are consistent with their understanding of the Christian faith. There has not been a long tradition or common practice of using Christian models of counselling in situations outside the church, so most Christian professionals do not use an overtly Christian approach to counselling, even though they may make clear the fact that they are themselves Christians.

INTEGRATION

The question we need to ask is - 'Is it possible for secular beliefs and practices to be satisfactorily integrated into a model of counselling which is compatible with a Christian approach?' There have been many arguments both for and against integration. Here we wish to outline some of the main points on both sides to allow readers to form their own opinion. However, it will not be difficult for you to tell what we think, so be prepared to balance our beliefs and preferably follow up some of the resources mentioned so that you may become better informed.

There are **three main concepts** or ideas which we need to explore before we can answer the question of whether integration is possible. These are:

> the common grace of God leading to a general revelation to all mankind;
> the meaning of truth;
> the models and theories of how men and women function both naturally and supernaturally.

1.   GENERAL REVELATION

It has been argued that there are two main sources of revelation. First, there is *special revelation* which is direct from God. Traditionally this has been seen as contained in the Bible. The second revelation is a *general revelation* which is given to all people and concerns the truth revealed in God's creation. A third and perhaps slightly more controversial form is also acknowledged where God speaks to us directly. This *personal revelation* is in reality a form of special revelation, which obviously cannot contradict God's other revelation through the Bible. For example God does not speak to people through personal revelation that they can marry someone who is already married, in contradiction of biblical principles.

The immediate problem with general revelation is that Paul seems to indicate that the un-spiritual man will misinterpret what he or she sees and hears.[1] However, it should also be pointed out that many Christians have also misinterpreted the Bible and come to conclusions which are against the widely held beliefs of the Church through the ages. The Bible stresses that all of us need the guidance of the Holy Spirit in order to interpret accurately

God's revelations to us.[2]

Some Christian psychologists will argue that it is quite acceptable for Christians to examine, analyse, select and then integrate practices from secular models. For example there is a well argued chapter contending just that in the book 'Introduction to Psychology and Counselling' by Paul Meier and Frank Minirth. [3] Figure 1 is an adaptation from the figure in their book.[4]

GOD
SOURCE OF ALL TRUTH

SPECIAL REVELATION
to Christians

GENERAL REVELATION
to all people

HERMENEUTICS
interpreting and
explaining the Bible

SCIENTIFIC METHOD
exploring and
explaining the world and
mankind through science

THEOLOGY

PSYCHOLOGY

ECLECTICISM
Analysing and comparing all approaches
and selecting the 'best bits' from each

Figure 1 Special and General Revelation - the relationship between Psychology and Theology

We would like to point out some of the problems associated with this process of selection and integration, which we feel are frequently minimised.

1. The process of integration assumes that the counsellor is seeking to integrate aspects of other counselling models in an eclectic approach, which selects and chooses aspects from many different theories and models. This requires choosing those elements to use and those to discard, and requires an able, mature and experienced person who is able to discern what is acceptable and helpful in any psychological theory and practice. Such a person clearly needs to be experienced in both psychology and theology. While some experts (such as Meier and Minirth) may well be able to do this, there is a danger that other, less experienced people, will be encouraged to undertake the same exercise, with sometimes less than satisfactory results.

2. Integration, for a Christian, demands that the special revelation of God takes precedence over what is understood to be his general revelation. Thus theology must take precedence over psychology. However, it is much more exacting to build a good model of counselling which is based on the Bible and completely consistent with theological truths. Basing a model on experience and observation is easier. Thus the psychological interpretation often triumphs over theology, and the danger is that the theology is made to fit in with the psychology. It is interesting that most secular theories of counselling are usually based on the experience and writings of just one or two men. In developing a Christian model, the counsellor is not only dependent on the revelation of the Holy Spirit, but also on the wisdom and criticism of other mature fellow Christians. The counsellor must be able to convince fellow Christians that this new understanding and approach is completely consistent with the Bible.

3. Terminology is often confusing, with non-Christians using

words and concepts in their counselling theory which have different meanings when used in the Bible. They then attach their own meanings to these words, so you may think you mean the same thing because the same words are used, but quite different concepts and interpretations may be given to the words, so causing confusion.

4. As pointed out previously, there have been very few Christian psychologists who have been widely accepted outside the Christian Church, because most of the assumptions of secular counselling and psychology are humanistic. As the methods used in counselling are closely linked to a theory of practice, it is difficult to see how parts of one method can be lifted out of the context of its original theory of practice and matched up with another theory of practice developed from a different belief system, without some distortion and tainting taking place. Christian models of counselling acknowledge that man is a spiritual being, created to function in relationship with God, but this is denied in all humanistic theories.

In summary we accept that there may be acceptable ways in which people who are experts can integrate parts of secular psychological and counselling practice into an effective Christian model, but it does require maturity and experience, both as a Christian and as a counsellor, to effect it in a safe and beneficial manner.

Some Christian authors argue very strongly against the integration of Christian and secular models of counselling, some of the best known being Larry Crabb,[5] and Martin and Deidre Bobgan.[6] Crabb has summed up his position.

'We must develop a solidly biblical approach to counselling, one which draws on secular psychology without betraying its Scriptural premise and which clings passionately and unswervingly to belief in an inerrant Bible and an all-sufficient Christ'.[7]

For a fuller discussion of this point see the books listed in endnotes 5,6 and 7on page 88.

2. TRUTH

One of the important concepts used in the debate about integration is the nature of *truth*, and so we should first consider what truth is. It may be correct to say, 'All truth is God's truth,' or, 'All truth is one,' but we perhaps need to consider whether there is more than one kind of truth.

We acknowledge as Christians that there is absolute truth - that which is true now, always has been true, and always will be true. However, in this life we cannot prove that this is true, so absolute truth must become an article of faith. Christians accept that absolute truth is an attribute of the triune God - he is the truth. Non-Christians also have a general understanding of a final and absolute truth, but recognise that it is impossible to find it in this world at this present time. Most people also believe in some sort of reference point beyond themselves, but rarely does it have an impact on their lives.

Thus most people recognise that a person's view of truth is based on his or her limited powers of observation and reasoning. A scientific truth may be defined as one which can be verified by direct observation and experiment. It is consistent, reproducible and always correct - until of course it is later proved false as our knowledge and understanding progresses. It may thus be considered a temporary truth which is at the peak of present knowledge. These truths should be called theories or models. There are no absolute truths in science. However, some *facts* are fairly certain, that is they have appeared to be true for a very long time. For example the fact that water boils at 100 degrees centigrade at sea level has always been confirmed to be true. Such facts are really observations of the world in which we live. Most people understand that our view of truth is limited to our senses and the limitations we have in exploring reality.

The way in which we observe and interpret the *facts* to a great extent depends on the views and beliefs of the observer. We see what we expect to see, and we often discover what we want to find. All scientists are aware of the difficulty of bias and prejudice which prevents you from seeing the evidence you did not expect or did not want to see. We should, however, be wary of the approach which says that because the originator of a theory or model of practice was ungodly, then all of that theory must also be ungodly. The truths discovered by Newton, Pythagoras or Einstein did not depend in any way on their religious beliefs. However, it is perhaps different when considering discoveries about how men and women behave as there is a great difference between human behaviour and the purely physical laws. Thus in the domain of human beings, the beliefs of the originators of the theories will to a greater or lesser extent affect the validity of the theory itself.

God's view of truth must be different to that held by people. God can apparently cope with different aspects of the same truth at the same time. To us they may appear to be contradictory, but they are in reality different facets of the character and ways of

God. Into this category come the miracles, which apparently contradict the laws of nature which God created, but they are consistent to God. In him it is not always either/or, but also/and.

There is also a view that moral truths vary according to the times and cultures in which people are born. Such a view states that what is acceptable and morally right is largely determined by the norms of the society into which we are born. As Christians, while not being at all judgmental of other people, we should always be prepared to stand for the fact that God's truth in the Bible is the only acceptable way to behave. We need to remember that there are parts of any culture which are on a collision course with the Bible - Western cultures as well as Eastern cultures. Some cultures that violate Scripture in one area are extremely supportive of it in others, but culture can never be a measure of truth. Counsellors should be aware that all secular theories are based on an observational or experimental understanding of how men and women behave. Such human theories will have many *untruths* within them, although it is extremely difficult to discern what is true and what is untrue.

The revolution in psychotherapy of the sixties and seventies led by such famous names as Carl Rogers and Abraham Maslow has been termed by some as 'liberation psychotherapy'. Its core assumptions were that human nature is intrinsically benign (neither good or bad) and that the institutions of our society and culture repress us causing mental health problems.

The relationship between the self and society is seen as basically negative. Therapists such as Rogers and Maslow would argue that we are born with essentially benign characteristics, and that social institutions such as the family, church and education, which they see as at least mildly coercive, tend to stultify the self. The result, they predict, is turning that person into what Carl Rogers termed a 'defensively oriented personality'.

Such anti-institutionalism leaves individuals pretty much stranded. If communal control makes an individual psychologically sick, the individual must achieve autonomy from culture and society. All inherited normative and moral demands must be rejected to cultivate and create one's self through what Maslow called self-actualization. The co-dependency movement, the contemporary offspring of liberation psychotherapy, defines all problems in living as a form of addiction defined as 'process addiction' - being pathologically oriented toward some external activities, something outside of oneself. Those afflicted get all of their identity and feelings about self from the addicting external activity. One can be addicted to any number of things which take away bad feelings about self - for example, addiction to emotional volatility, sex, or shopping. All life problems are redefined as unmanageable behaviour over which the self is powerless. Psychological health is often defined in such a way that people have to reject social institutions in order to be well.

As Christians we, naturally, disagree with this notion of original innocence as it contradicts biblical teaching on original sin. It is not difficult to see how erroneous philosophies result from starting at the wrong point. As repressive as some social taboos have been, they do have their positive influence. Social influence remains the only effective, informal tool available to a pluralistic society to assure the number of social renegades remains at a manageable level. This paranoia over social influence gives the individual precedence over the group - rubber-stamping selfishness and undermining any sense of community. Any society that gives priority to the actualisation of self-seekers won't be able to call itself a civilisation for long.

3. MODELS OF HUMAN BEINGS - WHO DO WE THINK WE ARE?

All practical activity depends on a philosophy or world view which contains the beliefs on which actions are based. In the area of counselling all such world views contain an explicit or implicit model of how men and women work. These models of human-kind will include beliefs as to what health is, how illness is caused, and what can be done to restore health.

Much of Western science and medicine has been built on a model of people which is largely, if not totally, a bio-physiological one. Thus illness is a physical entity, either coming from the outside world and invading the body, or a malfunctioning from within, which has a biological framework of reference and therefore needs a physical treatment to counteract it. Most doctors and health-care workers will also subscribe to a psycho-somatic model of human beings. Here it is acknowledged that men and women are more than physical beings, and the mind and emotions can also adversely affect the physical functioning. Thus psychiatrists may be able to help the person with a backache through psychotherapy when the physical therapy fails.

Only Christian counselling, from its assumptive basis, takes up the challenge of the effects of true guilt due to sin on a person's life. That is probably because only Christian counselling can pro-duce a satisfactory cure for the problem of spiritual 'dis-ease'. We need to acknowledge that the models of care in a counselling setting must spring from the belief systems which underlie it. Thus secular models and Christian models will always be dis-tinctly different.

4 CHRISTIAN MODELS - WHO DOES GOD THINK WE ARE?

Christians have one great advantage when it comes to understanding who we are - we can communicate with our creator and get a 'God's eye view' of our situation. God enables us to have an objective view of reality which is absent when we only communicate with other created beings. As we communicate more with God so we find that we can also communicate more intimately with other people, through our spirits, than we could unaided.

How do we learn about humanity? Each one of us asks this question to some extent or other, and today we are extremely fortunate (or should I say blessed), because we have many ways at our disposal:

We have an ancient oral tradition which became a written history describing how our ancestors dealt with the same questions we face. For Christians this includes the richest literature in the world, from the Bible right down through 6000 years of God/man history.

We have the thoughts of thousands of people over many thousands of years recorded for us to read. We can learn much from the intellectual struggles of honest men, even when they have failed to discover God (and we can still get into trouble).

We can 'put our heads together', and through a process of mutual stimulation and questioning we are able to arrive at thoughts and solutions which no one person on his or her own could achieve (for good or bad).

We can build theoretical models which in an abstract sense describe general principles about reality. These models can then be tested by observation and experimentation to verify their validity and usefulness.

If we are to build models which help us to understand and make sense of everything else we come into contact with, then we first need to build an acceptable and biblical model of men and women. As Christians we have the advantage of using the Bible as an external reference point - an absolute and objective standard against which we can measure our theories. However, we need to be aware that scholars, theologians and ordinary Christians can all disagree as to the interpretation of biblical passages and what they actually mean to us today. It may be helpful to review the five sources of information which are available to us as we develop theories, as they all must take their proper place if our theories and models are to be both accurate and useful. The five sources are: the Bible; direct revelation from God; communion with other Christians; Church history and tradition; and direct observation of the world.

THE BIBLE

The Bible must be seen as the authoritative word of God from which we extract the principles on which we must build our lives today. We who are alive at the start of the third millennium after Christ are extremely privileged with a rich variety of Bible translations available.

When using the Bible to build models of understanding it is vital to recognise the value of ALL scripture. We often forget that when

Jesus and Paul talk about scripture they are referring to what we now call the Old Testament. The New Testament builds upon the Old, and is not really understandable without seeing it in the context of the history of Israel, and the new phase of God's plan of salvation by the grafting in of the Gentiles into his body. Try to avoid building principles and practices on one or two scripture references alone. A principle which will be of value should be expounded and developed by reference to all parts of scripture.

DIRECT (PERSONAL) REVELATION FROM GOD

Throughout the ages Christians have understood that the words written in the Bible were inspired by God and may be used by each culture and within each generation to guide the reader to God's truth. However, we cannot do this un-aided. Scripture tells us that the Holy Spirit has been sent by God to guide us into truth (John 16:13) and as we read the words in the Bible we require the Holy Spirit to aid us in interpreting them so that they become the words of life and truth to us today. We understand the Bible not just by scholarship, but by a present relationship with Jesus and the presence of the Holy Spirit within us which, among other things, provides up with a spiritual 'hot-line' to God the Father. (John 14:23-26) We also know that no direct or personal revelation will ever contradict his written revelation, because God does not contradict Himself.

COMMUNION WITH OTHER CHRISTIANS

If we accept that by becoming a Christian we become part of a Body, we must also bear in mind Paul's exhortation that each part of the Body is different from the other parts, and so each needs the others.[8] We should also willingly accept that when it comes to discovering God's word for us today, we cannot adequately hear God in isolation. Certainly, in our day in - day out devotional life it is necessary for the individual to hear God alone and without reference to other Christians. But our overall life direction and our understanding of the heart and mind of God must be shared in fellowship with other Christians. Sharing what we think God is saying to us, and hearing what others believe he is saying to them is a vital safeguard. Too many cults and heresies develop when one or two strong minded individuals believe that they alone have heard God, and then force that word onto their followers who are not allowed to question what the 'leader' has said. Even in many ordinary Churches there is an unspoken assumption that only the leaders can hear God. God speaks to ALL his children.[9] And only as we all share what God is saying to us through our Bible readings and prayers can the Church truly hear God's word for today.

CHURCH HISTORY AND TRADITION

There is a tendency by some people to attach too great a weight to Church tradition, but there is also a deficiency when too little importance is attached to the thoughts and writings of Christians throughout the 2000 years of recent history. We are blessed by the volume and quality of written works which show us how saints and scholars throughout the centuries have heard God and interpreted the Bible. The traditional beliefs of the Churches have developed over the centuries through the study and challenge of various scholars and saints. It seems that each period of history develops another heresy. They didn't always 'get it right', but as heresies are exposed the knowledge enriches the church as others are able to learn from past mistakes. It may well be that, since the closing of the Bible canon we have gained a greater understanding of the character of God through wrestling with heresies and mistakes than any other exercise. If we jettison church history and tradition, we will waste a vast bank of knowledge.

DIRECT OBSERVATION OF THE WORLD

Non-Christians have, basically, limited themselves to scientific observation of the natural world and so it is little wonder that they say that it is the only valid method of investigation. When it is most effective, science trains people to observe natural phenomena objectively, attempting to avoid bias in what is observed. From the observations made, questions are then developed which the scientist hopes will be open to experimentation. Complicated methodologies have been developed as it is extremely difficult to determine cause and effect through experiments. For example it has recently been suggested that a raised blood pressure in adults may result from the amount of salt in the diet given to the new born infant. To actually test that this theory is correct is not easy, and numerous different approaches are used to try to isolate this one factor (of salt in the diet of a new born) from all the other possible causes of elevated blood pressure as adults.

If it is difficult deciding whether salt early in life causes high blood pressure later, imagine just how difficult it is to investigate the effect of the mother-child relationship in infancy to the development of mental illness in adult life. In all sociological and psychological investigations there is the added complication in that the personality and world-view of the investigator may influence the observations and measurements made, as well as affect how those observations are interpreted. Those who accept the Bible and Trinitarian interpretations on core issues can stabilise the world view factor against what most Christians accept as known truth.

ACCEPTABLE INTEGRATION?

Integration implies the joining together in harmony of two similar things. To integrate implies that the elements to be joined together complement and enhance one another. Two things can therefore only be integrated together if they have a high degree of similarity and are complementary. When looking at secular models of counselling, are we able to accurately discern what is true and what is false? How do we decide what can or cannot be integrated? Some people believe that unthinking integration is itself responsible for some of the problems in the history of the Church. For example is present day inter-faith activity within the church an example of integration of the worst sort? Are many of the heresies in Church history examples of wrong integration? Can you integrate together beliefs and practices which come from different world views?

It has been pointed out in studies of the way in which the Church developed in pagan societies such as Africa, that many converts were allowed to claim Christ without fully relinquishing the pagan and cultural beliefs to which they had previously clung. Frequently the beliefs and practices of Christianity were simply incorporated into an already existing doctrinal system, and the end result was often more pagan than Christian. In these cases integration was a disaster and has held back the growth of the Christian church in many countries.

Many of the philosophies, belief systems and assumptions of psychoanalysis are opposed to those of Christianity. How can these two then be integrated? If we have two different models, how can we integrate - which is defined as 'to make one'? There are sincere Christian counsellors on both sides of this argument, and we would urge the student to read widely and keep an open mind on this subject, while at all times asking God for wisdom to be able to discern between helpful beliefs and practice, and those which might produce harm.

BUILDING BIBLICAL MODELS

There is no space in this introductory text to describe or evaluate the many different models of human beings that have been proposed. Any model of counselling will have to develop a model to inform its methodology, but in Christian counselling there is a common framework upon which all are based. Let us describe a hypothetical case study to see how to develop and use such a model.

Jane is now in her early thirties and has been married for seven years to Tom. They were not Christians when they married, but three years ago Jane became a Christian during a local mission, although Tom did not. There has been some tension over this, but Tom let Jane get on with her church going while he followed his old interests. Recently Jane has been worried that Tom is less affectionate and may be seeing another women. She becomes depressed and does not want to go out. Tom doesn't understand what is going on inside her, and anyway finds her less attractive now. Jane begins to develop blinding headaches and sees her doctor who diagnoses migraine. He prescribes a course of tablets to help. Jane now has feelings of despair, is in considerable pain with her headaches, and has stopped going to Church as she feels that God is unable to help in her situation as she has prayed but received no relief. The minister at her Church said that she must be prepared to admit that sin in her life must be at the root of the problem, and if she prayed in faith she would be healed. In despair she tries to commit suicide with an overdose of tablets. Tom decides to leave her and ask for a divorce. You are asked to see Jane and provide counselling. What is wrong with her?

Clearly Jane has physical problems - the headaches of migraine can be disabling. She has emotional and mental problems with her depression, and she has spiritual problems with her damaged faith and view of God. The essence of the Christian view is that each person is a whole. All parts work together and if one part is ill then the other parts become ill as well. The doctor will approach the problem from the physical symptoms and seek to help the headache. He may also advise that Jane sees a psychiatrist to explore the depression that has developed. The minister believes that the problem is a lack of faith, and if Jane confessed her sins and prayed in faith then she would be healed. A marriage guidance counsellor would point to the strained relationship as the cause of the problem. All of these may be right in a limited sense, for all of these aspects of Jane's life are affected.

From a consideration of this case we might conclude:

Each person is a unified whole - when one part of the person is affected, all the others become affected also.

Ill health can start in the body, in the mind, in the emotions, or in the spirit.

Most problems have multiple causes, which unite together to produce sickness.

Help for such sickness needs to address all the component factors.

Thus with Jane we need to provide physical help for her pain, and possibly anti-depressants to prevent another suicide attempt. She needs counselling over her reactions to her husband, and they will require help as a couple if the marriage is to be saved. She needs spiritual help to understand how God can help her, and above all she needs loving support through a very stressful period. To be effective all of these therapies need to be coordinated. It is often the Christian counsellor who can best take this role.

CONCLUSIONS

In summary we would like to stress the following points -

1 All of the humanistic models of counselling have some validity, and in most cases are utilised by sincere people who seek the very best for the people in need who come to them.

2 Many counsellors seek to take the best from different models of counselling and apply them in a way they have found helpful. Many clients have thus benefited from secular counselling.

3 However, all of the humanistic theories of counselling deny the existence and relevance of God, and his absolute truth. In one way or another they rely on the human power within a person to effect change. See page 268 in Appendix A

4 Care needs to be taken when seeking to integrate secular methods into a Christian approach to counselling. The Christian model alone can incorporate the true benefits of secular methods with the additional bonus of acknowledging God and his part in any healing process.

CHAPTER END NOTES

[1]. Romans 1:21-22 [2]. John 16:13

[3]. *Introduction To Psychology and Counselling* by Paul Meier, Frank Minirth, Frank Wichen and Donald Ratcliffe. Published by Monarch Books, Tunbridge Wells, England 1991 (Second edition of book first published in 1982 by Baker Book House Company)

[4]. Ibid page 30, this figure is itself an adaptation from one in the book 'The Bible in counselling' by W Ward).

[5].*Basic Principles of Biblical Counselling*, Larry Crabb published originally by Zondervan in 1975. British edition published by Marshalls in 1985

[6]. *The Psychological Way, The Spiritual Way* by Martin and Deidre Bobgan. Published by Bethany House Publishers, Minneapolis, USA 1979

[7].*Basic Principles of Biblical Counselling* by Lawrence Crabb, published by Marshalls, Basingstoke in 1985 p 20

[8]. Ephesians 4:25 and 1 Corinthians 11:12-27

[9]. John 10:3-4

APPROACHES TO CHRISTIAN COUNSELLING

There have been many different approaches to a Christian model of counselling in recent years. An overview of the history and development of the main models of Christian counselling has been well described by Roger Hurding in *Roots and Shoots*,[1] and the serious student should spend time in his book. We strongly advise students who intend working within the ministry of counselling to read and explore further into those models which appear to be relevant to their needs. At the end of this chapter you will find a table summarising the main Christian counselling models which may be encountered. Obviously, you will find some more Christian than others.

GUIDELINES FOR CHRISTIAN COUNSELLORS

There are numerous models of Christian counselling and then there are many individual variations and personal combinations. Each approach is based on an understanding of how human beings function, and how God, through the Holy Spirit, works to bring health and wholeness. It is also valid for Christians to construct their own theoretical models on which they will build their practice. But there are guidelines and key concepts which we need to agree that all counsellors should adhere to.

The client must be respected, and their beliefs recognised. At the heart of most models is an understanding that the integrity of the client is of paramount importance. However, most models also acknowledge that the belief system of the client is often faulty, and help is given to enable the client to correct their belief systems. The adjustments necessary to make these corrections are defined by the counsellor - a big responsibility. For counselling to be Christian it must be underpinned by a basic doctrine of God, Jesus and the Holy Spirit which has been central to main-line churches for nearly 2000 years. This will frequently be in direct conflict with many of the values, morals and behaviour which will be encountered in counselling relationships. We acknowledge variations from one denomination to the next, but the core beliefs are the same. Counsellors must learn to refer to these core beliefs in 'neutral' language. For instance, all mainline denominations believe in the 'filling of the Spirit', but when the term 'baptism of the Spirit' is substituted it becomes a 'trigger word' in some circles. The Evangelical Alliance statement of faith is widely accepted by many churches, although many Anglicans and Catholics may differ over one or two points or emphases. We are seeking to emphasise that which unites us rather than that which divides.

Counsellors should be transparent as to their own beliefs and when they share their own thoughts and experiences the clients should be able to understand what the counsellors words and attitudes are based on. We need to recognise that the beliefs of the counsellor will always affect any counselling interaction, and the Christian counsellor needs to find ways of clearly indicating that although they hold particular views there are also other views. Above all we need to avoid the dogmatic Christian counsellor who *knows* that he or she knows the truth and their duty is to make the client also believe it.

It is argued by many that the counsellor should never seek to 'direct' a client. Of course some methods of Christian counselling are much more directive than others. As we have already discussed there is probably no such thing as completely non-directive counselling as in any interaction one person will almost certainly affect the other even if they try not to. Our attitudes and beliefs can be expressed involuntarily even if we say absolutely nothing. However, there are degrees of directiveness, and we recommend that the counsellor should always seek to minimise the influence they exert over the client so that the thoughts, attitudes and decisions made are indeed the client's own.

In certain circumstances it may be valid for the counsellor to give advice to the client, but this should be couched in such a way that the various options are clearly presented. Encouragement should be given to clients for them to make their own choices, and it should be stressed that the counselling relationship does not depend on the client's choices conforming to those of the counsellor, otherwise this exerts an undue pressure to conform to the counsellor's wishes.

The counsellor will continue to help the client even if they disagree with the beliefs of the counsellor so long as the client is benefiting and wishing to continue. However, counselling involves a two way relationship and a point may well be reached where the counsellor should honestly challenge the client as to whether any useful purpose is served in continuing a therapeutic relationship where the beliefs are radically different.

TEN STEPS OF CHRISTIAN COUNSELLING

Most models of Christian counselling will have much in common. We can summarise the core of Christian counselling in the following ten step approach. Every counselling approach which follows a Christian model should have most or all of the following steps contained within them:-

1. PROVIDING A SAFE RELATIONSHIP

The counsellor starts by building a relationship based on trust and acceptance which enables the client to open up their hearts in a safe environment in which his or her confidences will be respected.

2. BEFRIEND, COME ALONGSIDE

The Christian counsellor, acting as the channel for God's love, comes alongside the client, to provide support and encouragement. This process of befriending involves some degree of involvement in the life of the client, although, of course, the counsellor should always be aware of the danger of making the client too dependant on them.

3. CREATIVE LISTENING

The counsellor uses listening skills to hear and understand the problems the client has, and at the same time hears and experiences in a small way God's heart for the person. It's helpful to remember the saying 'this is why God gave us two ears - so that with one we could listen to people, and with the other listen to God.'

4. UNDERSTANDING

However it is done, the counsellor seeks to gain understanding and insight into the client's life and problems. While this may involve our ability to use our God-given faculties to understand, we believe it also involves a spiritual perception to gain understanding from God's point of view. While some counsellors believe that it is important to have sympathy for the client, and others believe that empathy is vital (which may be defined as - I share the experience of your pain in my heart), we believe that an even higher level of understanding is when we have compassion for the person we are helping. God's compassion was essential during the ministry of Jesus,[2] and it should also be important for us. We need to recognise God's pain for the person in order to have a God-centred view of the problem rather than just a person-centred view.

5. COUNSEL GOD'S TRUTH AND CHARACTER WITH WISDOM

To provide Christian counsel does imply the imparting of some aspects of truth concerning God and his ways. This needs to be done with wisdom (again preferably a God-given wisdom rather than one based solely on one's own experience), which perceives when and how to speak, and when to keep silent. The gift of wisdom is one of the gifts of the Holy Spirit to us in order to help people. [3]

6. CONFRONTATION BY JESUS

At the heart of the counselling process - and the key to all Christian counselling - is the confrontation between the person being counselled and the living God. When humans confront, it is often destructive, leading to division or disintegration. But when the loving Father confronts in love, it admittedly produces pain, but it is constructive in that it builds up and heals the person as well.[4] All secular counselling and psychological methods can discover much of what is wrong with a person. They can confront a person with aspects of the truth, but it is only if this *holy confrontation* takes place that the person can be put back together again. The power for people to change comes from God.[5] God may use us as the counsellor's assistant in this process of confrontation, but we must be conscious that God comes in his own time and his own way. We should not try to force people, but lovingly support, encourage and challenge as led by the Holy Spirit until this confrontation takes place.

7. AFFIRMATION AND INTEGRATION

Following the confrontation which occurs when God speaks directly to a person, there needs to be a time of affirmation and clarification. Any meeting with God is daunting and is frequently followed by doubts. Did anything really happen? Was that God or just my imagination? The task of the counsellor is to talk through the encounter helping the client to understand what happened and what God has said and done. Confusion needs to be dealt with, and a clear distinction made between the words of God and the additions and interpretations we all use to embroider and develop what God says to us. The counsellor stresses the hope of future change and the need to put God's words into action.

8. ACTION AND APPLICATION

The counsellor encourages the client to begin to put into practice what they have learned. You may use homework assignments, or group therapy, or a variety of ways of helping the person to apply truth they have received into their lives. This is the hardest and most time consuming part of counselling, and should lead naturally into a discipling process where the clients continue to work out their problem within the context of normal relationships and activities.

9. PROVIDING SUPPORT

The counsellor should commit to continuing to help and support the client for as long as he or she needs it. This may be through personal contact, or through referral to others, backed up by concern to support in prayer. So many people find that they slip back after counselling, and usually a short period of encouragement from the counsellor can help them on their way again.

10. RELEASE INTO MINISTRY

We should never forget that the end point of all ministry is to help people to maturity in Christ,[6] the end result of which is to release them into valid and constructive ministry. Our aim is not to make people happy, nor to make them content with themselves. Rather it is to build them up so that they may be equipped to go out and help others. This task of training and equipping will usually not be carried out by the counsellor, but Christian counselling is an integral part of the great commission.

THE MIKDAV WINDOW

At this point we need to raise the issue of a counsellor's style and approach to counselling when faced with the differing needs of clients. To do this we will use the Mikdav window which represents the changing counselling style which is appropriate to the emotional and mental state of the client as counselling progresses.

EMOTIONAL STABILITY

The vertical axis of the window is a continuum representing the client's emotional and mental stability. At the extreme bottom end of the scale will be a person who has been hurt, and is unable to face reality. They will be in a very fragile state, easily upset and tearful. They are unstable.

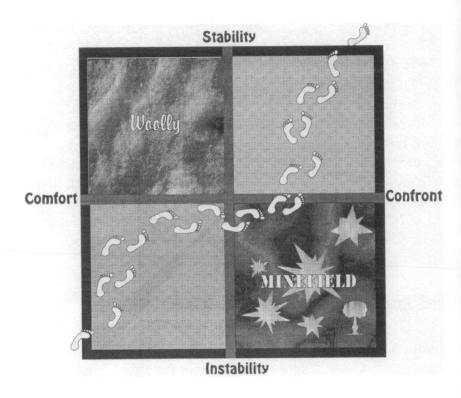

At the top end of the scale will be a person who is 'stable' in their mental and emotional state. They are able to accept reality and truth. They may have some emotional disturbance because of the nature of the problems faced, but nevertheless are able to accept it, and have the strength and ability to work at issues.

COUNSELLING STYLE

The horizontal continuum represents what might be considered counselling style. At the extreme left of the scale will be the completely non-directive approach, where most of the activity is comforting and calming the hurt person and pouring balm onto their wounds. A process of binding up and comforting would typify the effects of the actions taken. Obviously, this stage lays the groundwork for later healing and constructive work.

At the right end of the scale is the confrontational and more directive style. Here the client is challenged and confronted with truth and reality in a way that they can work with the counsellor to achieve the desired growth and change.

These two continuum lines form four 'windows' of style into which the counsellor and client may move during counselling sessions.

1. COMFORTING - UNSTABLE

The bottom left hand-window is the appropriate place to start when the client is unstable and hurting. The first action of the counsellor is to provide care and empathy to the person who is hurt, confused and often emotionally unstable. Of course, we comfort with God's comfort and not just with our own sympathy. An empathy needs to be built up so that the client trusts the counsellor, and understands that God also comforts us with his compassion and love at the same time as he seeks for our healing and growth.

As the client progresses they gradually move upwards and their new strength means that they are able to accept a more challenging view of their situation. The persuasion of God's wisdom is at the heart of Christian Counselling, and is what distinguishes it from all other counselling models. God's truth, as revealed in Christ and contained in the Bible, forms the framework of reality against which clients need to measure their thoughts, feelings, attitudes and behaviour.

2. CHALLENGING - STABLE

The top right-hand window is the place where all counselling should aim for. Here the client has reached a more stable mental and emotional state, and the counselling therefore may be more challenging. The ability to challenge and confront in a way that produces a positive response and therefore growth is the hallmark of a mature Christian counsellor. This stage is probably the most misunderstood and abused. It is God who challenges and confronts us, and if the counsellor is not in close communion with God then any confrontation can be fleshly and counterproductive.

This final stage of counselling is the most exciting, because here the client and counsellor are working together with the Holy Spirit to bring about the desired growth in feelings, thoughts, attitudes and behaviour.

There are two *dangerous* windows into which we should take great care not to stray.

3. THE MINEFIELD

The bottom right-hand window brings a more confrontational counselling style with a client who is still unstable. It is clearly inappropriate for a counsellor to adopt a confronting posture while the client is hurt and confused. The result could well be a breakdown in the relationship and a client who is worse off than before. With a mentally unstable person there is a danger of the client damaging themselves, including an increased risk of suicide.

4. WOOLLY

The top left-hand window is another danger area where the counselling style remains comforting and non-challenging when the client is recovering their mental and emotional stability, and so is in a position to face reality and work through the issues in their life. If the counsellor and client silently collude to not face issues then a degree of **dependence** may develop, and both parties may come to enjoy a relationship and a process which becomes an end in itself. Stagnation is the dangerous state in which the client ceases to grow or become whole because of a fear of the pain which is required for growth to occur. If a client reaches complete stability in this area he has done so in spite of the counselling received after he reached the mid point of the chart and not as a result of it.

This necessarily brief introduction to the core beliefs and practices of Christian counselling, allied to an outline of some of the more common approaches, should now enable the student to begin sitting with experienced counsellors to observe how they help people.

A COUNSELLING MODEL ILLUSTRATION

The numerous variations in Christian counselling models seem to have more to do with the integration of psychology into the model rather than churchmanship. One might expect there to be a correlation between regard for Scripture and the degree to which psychology is integrated into counselling methods. This is true to a point, but not to the degree that might be expected, because many see psychology as a pure science and therefore devoid of any values.

We think it would be helpful to look at the structure, usage and thinking behind one well respected Christian model.

Many of Larry Crabb's books refer to certain crucial longings deep down in every human. He specifically looks at longings for *security and significance*. Security - the knowledge that we are loved with a love that doesn't have to be earned and therefore cannot be lost. Significance - the knowledge that our life has some amount of positive impact. He points out that these crucial longings are met in Christ for all who bear his image. His counselling model centres around the proposition that human problems emerge from our attempts to have these longings fulfilled by means other than through Christ. Rather than focus on our identity as image bearers, our attitudes and actions declare our independence. In order to explore the whole person he segments human attributes into four categories or circles and then explores these circles one by one.

Selwyn Hughes, the founder of CWR, adds one more circle to Larry Crabb's four which would create an image reminiscent of the Olympic logo were it not for the fact that they are generally pictured in bull's-eye fashion. His central circle is the human spirit, then moving outwards are the rational, volitional, emotional and finally the physical circle. (See diagram) Hughes includes self-worth in his list of crucial needs, and maintains that human problems are the result of attempts to gain security, significance and self-worth independently of God. Both Selwyn Hughes and Larry

Crabb base their models on the supremacy of Scripture. Certain psychological insights may be integrated into their counselling models but Scripture is the final authority.

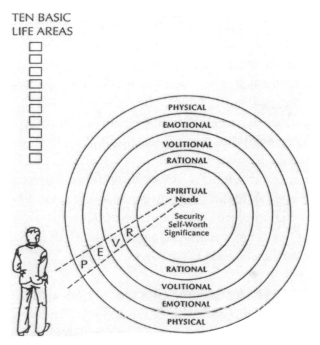

TEN BASIC
LIFE AREAS

PHYSICAL
EMOTIONAL
VOLITIONAL
RATIONAL

SPIRITUAL
Needs

Security
Self-Worth
Significance

RATIONAL
VOLITIONAL
EMOTIONAL
PHYSICAL

CWR's methodology suggests three phases of counselling: exploring the problem, diagnosing the cause and applying solutions. The first stage, exploring the problem involves another bit of structure known as *The Ten Basic Life Areas* which look at:

        family background
        social/emotional background
        current family/social relationships
        occupation and academic background
        finances
        spiritual life
        sexual activity

          recreation and leisure
          physical health
          routine responsibilities.

Having obtained as complete a picture as possible of the presenting problem, the counsellor is then equipped to enter phase two with some sort of tentative diagnosis. The counsellor can then begin to move through the five circles. The initial approach is through the physical circle which attempts to rule out the possibility of any medical condition which could be affecting the situation. This is probably the least threatening place to start.

Then the counsellor would move on to explore the emotions - what are the client's feelings about the problem. This would not be limited to the presenting problem. The counsellor would also have in mind his or her tentative diagnosis and form questions to explore circumstances linked with that.

In the volitional circle the counsellor would want answers to the question: 'What are the goals this client has set?' This speculates that the client has, consciously or unconsciously, made certain assumptions about a specific way to satisfy one or more of his crucial needs, for a rather simplistic example, 'I will hold the floor with a lot of witty stories and jokes so that people will see me as significant.'

The rational circle explores the thinking behind the goals. There is a good possibility that the client is thinking something like: 'People receiving the greatest amount of attention are the most significant. Therefore, gaining attention is the fastest route to significance.' Note, as this is the diagnostic phase, normally, no attempt to correct or challenge this thinking would normally be made.

The fifth circle - the spiritual - is the segment where crucial longings are addressed. By gentle probing both the counsellor and the client are able to discover what the client has been depending on for his sense of value. Completing statements such as; 'I felt worthwhile when...' make good facilitators. A bit of teaching may be called for to make the client aware of these basic longings and the fact that they are met in Christ. The counsellor would then share his or her diagnosis with the client.

It must be noted that work in this spirit circle is precarious, as the goal of the session is to assist the client in facing the subjective reality of unfulfilled longings. Coming to grips with the devices we employ to have our needs met is very painful. However, once the client has identified his misplaced dependency and/or independent spirit he or she is well equipped to make full and complete repentance. CWR training cautions that entering the spiritual circle should never be attempted without sufficient time to complete that phase in the same session.

Having entered the spiritual circle in the diagnostic phase, the counsellor starts phase three, which is the application stage. The teaching on longings needs to be reinforced to take the client beyond the discovery that the things and people he has been depending on can never fully satisfy these longings. He will need to know what the Bible teaches about his security, self-worth and significance being made complete in Christ. The client will also need to understand the necessity of entering into deep and meaningful repentance as sin is excluding God from the central part of his or her being.

Going back out through the rational circle the counsellor would re-identify and correct any wrong beliefs. Wrong thinking is the basis of inappropriate goals. Here is an area where the CWR model encourages the appropriate use of a secular technique. They recommend the use of the Albert Ellis' ABC concept. Where A = activating event, B = belief about the event and C = consequent emotion. In other words A has not engendered C, but rather B, which is what we believe about A. This is particularly helpful in helping clients rethink some painful childhood events.

In the volitional circle the client is encouraged to develop right goals and to behave accordingly.

In the emotional circle the client is taught how to deal with future negative emotions - to face them, to feel them and to attempt to discover their origin. Also to express negative emotions in harmony with God's purposes.

And finally, departing the case through the physical circle the counsellor would encourage the client to be a good steward of God's property. To pay attention to such things as exercise and diet.

Both Selwyn Hughes and Larry Crabb believe that psychological insights and techniques can be employed where they carry no moral values, but they must still be subject to the light of Scripture.

IN CLOSING

Remember that God is always the same for each person, but each person is unique. This means that God's answers for each person and each situation will also be unique. However much of a strict protocol we try to follow, God cannot be confined to our methods. He often delights to surprise and confound us. But when God does challenge a client we should be able to instantly recognise that this is God. Spiritual discernment is a vital gift for the Christian counsellor. Sometimes people are confused as to whether a particular manifestation or occurrence is from God, made up by the person themselves, or even from Satan.

We need to recognise that Satan and some human beings will try to 'fake' God's voice at times.[7] This emphasises the importance of the Christian counsellor being a mature Christian in open fellowship with other Christians with whom he or she can pray and discuss. At the end of the day, we often have to trust that God is in control, and as long as we are always seeking to follow God then we will not go far wrong.

This table summarises some of the common models of Christian counselling in use today. It is by no means complete, but gives an overview of the wide variety of approaches avaliable. Some of the names of the counselling models are taken from *Roots and Shoots* by Roger Hurding.

COUNSELLING MODEL	Main people involved in developing model	Notes and useful reading
Biblical counselling	Larry Crabb	Lawrence Crabb has written several books such as *Basic principles of Biblical counselling*, and *Effective Biblical counselling.*
	Selwyn Hughes and CWR	Selwyn Hughes has written The *Christian counsellor's pocket guide* as well as several counselling courses taught by CWR
Noethetic counselling	Jay Adams	A good introduction to Jay Adams is *Competent to Counsel* or *The Christian Counsellor's Manual*

COUNSELLING MODEL	Main people involved in developing model	Notes and useful reading
Spiritual counselling	Martin and Deidre Bobgan	*How to Counsel from Scripture* by Martin and Deidre Bobgan
Inner Healing	John and Paula Sandford	Books by John and Paula Sandford such as *The Transformation of the Inner Man* and *Healing the Wounded Spirit*
Inner Healing	Matthew and Dennis Linn	*Healing Life's Hurts* Dennis and Matthew by Linn
	Trevor Dearing	*God and Healing of the Mind* by Trevor Dearing
Discipleship Counselling	Gary Collins & Gary Sweeten	*Christian Counselling* by Gary Collins *Discipleship Counselling manual* by Gary Sweeten
Relationship counselling	Howard Clinebell	Basic Types of Pastoral Care and Counselling by Howard Clinebell
	Paul Tournier	Paul Tournier has written several books such as *A Doctor's Casebook in the Light of the Bible* Gary Collins has written T*he Christian Psychology of Paul Tournier*
Prayer counselling	Bruce Thompson	Based on the Divine Plumbline ministry of Dr Thompson. He has written *Walls of My Heart*
	Leanne Payne	Ministry through healing prayer. Books by Leanne Payne include *The Broken Image* and *The Healing Presence*
Clinical Theology	Frank Lake	A theological and psychological approach to clinical pastoral care. *Clinical Theology* by Frank Lake, abridged by Martin Yeomans, 1986

COUNSELLING MODEL	Main people involved in	Notes and useful reading
Christian Psychology	David Myers and Malcolm Jeeves Minerth and Meiers	*Psychology Through the Eyes of Faith* by Myers and Jeeves *Introduction to Psychology and Counselling* by Paul Meier, Frank Minirth, Frank Wichen and Donald Ratcliffe.
Deliverance ministry	Graham Powell	Counselling by concentrating on deliverance ministry has been described in *Christian Set Yourself Free* by Graham Powell,
Christian career Counselling	Arthur Miller and Ralph Mattson	*The Truth About You* by Miller Mattson discuss your motivated abilities.
	Gordon and Rosemary Jones	*Naturally Gifted* by Gordon and Rosemary Jones

END OF CHAPTER NOTES

1. *Roots and Shoots*, Roger Hurding, Hodder and Stoughton, London 1985
2. Matthew 14:14
3. 1 Corinthians 12:8
4. Hebrews 12: 10-11
5. 2 Peter 1:3
6. Romans 8:29
7. 2 Corinthians 11:14

THE CORE SKILLS OF COUNSELLING

COUNSELLING SKILLS

Many of the core skills used by counsellors are similar, no matter what method or model of counselling is used. There is a large amount of overlap between secular and Christian counselling in the initial stages, however a wide divergence in the skills required and the techniques used becomes apparent as the counselling therapy progresses. In this chapter we deal with those basic skills of counselling which should be used by everyone, no matter what model is being followed. In chapter 8 we discuss the specific skills involved in most models of Christian counselling, and in chapter 9 we discuss the practical issues which need to be addressed by anyone taking the counselling ministry seriously. We describe all of these skills and attributes from the viewpoint of the Christian counsellor. The Christian approach of counselling is unique and complete, while many of the skills are similar to those used in the main secular models.

CORE SKILLS

It is widely accepted that there is a collection of basic skills which are common to all types of counselling. These core skills combine attributes of the counsellor themselves, their personality and attitudes, as well as the essential skills of communication which are the foundation of counselling therapy.

These basic skills will be examined in this chapter under the following headings.

1 The attributes of the counsellor.
2 The setting of the counselling contract.
3 Making first contacts with clients.
4 Forming relationships.
5 Listening and questioning.
6 Gaining insight and understanding.
7 Assessment of people and their problems.
8 Building a deeper level of understanding.

1. THE ATTRIBUTES OF THE COUNSELLOR

Counselling is a calling and should be seen as a ministry in which the counsellor seeks to bring the power of the Holy Spirit into the person's situation. Not everyone is gifted to be a counsellor. We all have different personalities and needs, so it is important for the potential counsellor to closely examine their motives for entering this ministry.

THE COUNSELLOR'S MOTIVATION

A sincere desire to help people is of course a valid reason for becoming a counsellor. Other reasons, sometimes unrecognised, can interfere with the counsellor's effectiveness.

There are many *wrong motivations* for counselling. Those people who have an unhelpfully strong need for the following should normally be encouraged to avoid attempting to help others until they themselves have received counsel:

>**THE NEED FOR RELATIONSHIPS** - or the need to be needed.

>**THE NEED FOR CONTROL** - the authoritarian person who needs to 'straighten out' other people.

>**THE NEED TO RESCUE AND SAVE OTHER PEOPLE** - the hero.

>**THE NEED FOR INFORMATION** - being too curious, with a tendency to gossip.

>**THE NEED FOR PERSONAL HEALING** - carrying an overload of hidden needs and insecurities.

It is probable that every prospective counsellor will experience some of these tendencies at times, but such needs must be dealt with in situations apart from our work with counsellees.

POSITIVE ATTRIBUTES NEEDED FOR COUNSELLING

What are the positive attributes of the counsellor which will need to be developed and matured? We can sum them up under the following qualities.

>**GENUINENESS AND WARMTH**. This phrase is often used by secular counsellors to signify a person who is secure in themselves and able to be genuine with people without falling into the two extremes of either an embarrassing and inappropriate

openness about their own personal problems on the one hand, or withdrawal and hiding behind a facade on the other. Counsellors need to exude a natural friendliness and have genuine concern about other people, no matter who they are or what problems they may have.

INTEGRITY AND HONESTY. The counsellor needs to acknowledge his or her own difficulties and doubts. Alongside this goes a need for *HUMILITY.* It is so easy to assume that you are right and the other person wrong. This goes especially for beliefs and interpretations of scripture. A willingness to hold one's tongue and accept that the other person may well be right needs to be cultivated.

OPENNESS AND VULNERABILITY. These qualities denote a willingness to share and discuss areas where the counsellor may also have problems. Some degree of mutual sharing is usually needed in a counselling relationship. Some counsellor training doesn't allow for this. One counsellor said 'I never "get in the ring" with the counsellee'. But that is exactly what the incarnation is all about - God got into the ring with his fallen creation. It is not always possible or advisable to share your own failures with a client, but when and if it can be done, it pays great dividends in creating trust. Many clients have a distorted notion that counsellors are far more self-controlled, godly and intelligent than they are. Far from losing credibility, shattering this myth may actually establish credibility and give hope. Some counsellors, ourselves included, have made a pact with God that they will share anything with a client that they believe will be of help.

PATIENCE AND COMMITMENT. Many clients will need an extended time to fully recover from their problems. The counsellor must learn not to rush people, or try to speed up God's timing. Also it is usual for the client to fall back after a series of counselling sessions and come to the counselling session with words like - 'It's no good, I'm worse than before I started, it will never get better'. The ability to pick up such situations and get the person back on their feet is one of the hallmarks of a good counsellor.

Mature Christian. It goes without saying that a Christian counsellor must be a mature Christian and in on-going open fellowship with other Christians. However, we have been surprised at the number of 'lone rangers' who believe that God has called them to help people, but are unable to sustain relationships with other Christians. Christian maturity will include:

• *A SOLID GRASP OF BIBLICAL TRUTH.* Being secure in your own faith, not threatened by the doubts and attitudes of others who are struggling in their faith. This also implies an ability to sensitively deal with anger and frustration in others without over-responding yourself.

• *BEING A GENUINE SEEKER AFTER GOD,* not giving up on suitable periods of personal devotion, remembering that personal renewal and refreshment is not an optional extra but an essential requirement for a lifetime of effective ministry.

• *BEING IN OPEN AND ACCOUNTABLE RELATIONSHIPS.* In short, being under authority.

• *BEING TEACHABLE AND OPEN TO CORRECTION.* Always being able to learn from each new person and situation.

• *HAVING GOD'S HEART OF COMPASSION* for others and the heart desire to be a channel for God's mercy to hurting people.

• *WISDOM GAINED THROUGH EXPERIENCE.* Being able to translate one's own experiences, with God's help, into a growing understanding of God's ways and wisdom. This does not mean that the counsellor has to have suffered in the same way as the client has. In fact this can have certain drawbacks. The counsellor who has themselves suffered in similar ways to their client, may assume that the way in which they themselves found help must also be the best way for their clients. This means that they can consciously or unconsciously direct the client along a similar pathway. Having said all that, I (Dave) have found the fact that we lost a son in a car crash does give Joyce and me certain qualifications we wouldn't otherwise have - credibility in certain situations if nothing else.

GIFTED OR TRAINED?

We believe that people with personality profiles which major on being able to form relationships and have a natural compassion for people with problems will find it easier to become counsellors. However, anyone who believes God has called them can develop their personalities and skills to be used of God in counselling. People are going to be most comfortable when functioning within the area of their gifts. God's calling to counsel may be temporary or a special equipping for certain circumstances. Neither of us believe we are particularly gifted as counsellors, our gifts are more in teaching where a certain amount of counselling is inevitable, and as a result we have done a fair amount of counselling.

2. THE SETTING OF THE COUNSELLING CONTRACT

Many Christians assume that because counselling may be seen as part of a pastoral process that making contracts and keeping records is something to be avoided. We *counsel* you against this attitude. A good pastor will keep his own records to chart the problems and progression of his flock. There is also a clear contract within most churches which lays out the ethics, responsibilities and duties of the pastor. The counsellor needs to examine with the client all aspects of the nature of the counselling situation before they begin.

THE MAIN ELEMENTS OF THE COUNSELLING SETTING WILL INCLUDE -

WHO IS DOING THE COUNSELLING? Most counselling will take place in a one-to-one setting, although it is also common for there to be two counsellors during some or all sessions. This would often occur in training situations and in marriage counselling. The client needs to be given a reasonable choice as to the number and gender of counsellors, but if their choice cannot be met the counsellor should offer to go ahead, and if required in the future refer the client to another counsellor of the preferred gender. The competence and experience of the counsellor should also be communicated to the client. The code of ethics followed by the counsellor should be available or given to the client, and should always include details of how complaints may be raised if the client is hurt by the counselling relationship. We would expect all regularly practising Christian counsellors to be accredited or seeking accreditation with the Association of Christian Counsellors (ACC) or another equivalent body.

THE ACCOUNTABILITY OF THE COUNSELLOR. The client should understand that the counsellor is accountable to a director of the counselling service or pastor (depending on the setting) , and must also be in a supervision arrangement with a recognised supervisor.

THE TYPE OF COUNSELLING TO BE USED. A written statement concerning the model of counselling to be used is always helpful. Each counsellor should prepare a simple one page statement which outlines the component activities of the model (or models) of counselling which they will use.

THE BOUNDARIES OF THE COUNSELLING ACTIVITY. It is necessary for counsellors to have an agenda for his or her time with the client. This assures direction, efficiency, understanding and gives some guarantee that it is the counsellor who is actually in the driver's seat. This agenda should take the counsellee's expectations into consideration so it is somewhat of a joint effort. The client should be encouraged to verbalise specific objectives for the counselling. What are the topics they particularly want to address? What are their concerns, fears and what might they perceive as un-met needs?

THE COUNSELLORS' AGENDA is to make sure that they and the client are both playing by the same rule book. Some Christians may need to be reminded that God is usually not in the quick fix-it business. There is evidence in the Bible that he specifically uses life problems for producing growth and maturity in people. Good examples which can be used as homework assignments include studies of the lives of such biblical characters as Joseph, Moses, David, Paul, Mark and Peter. God's objective is for believers to develop the character of

Christ and most of this is taught through the problems we encounter. Successful counselling depends on both the client and the counsellor co-operating with God to discern how their current difficulties blend with his eternal objectives.

MAKING A CONTRACT. Whether you like it or not, a contract is made at the beginning of a counselling relationship. The expectations of the client and the counsellor are likely to be different and almost certain to cause conflict and pain in the future. It may seem almost callous to begin a counselling relationship talking about contracts - but once you get into the habit it is much easier.

It is not necessary to establish a contract in writing although many counsellors do. A contract is simply an agreement between two people and having it in writing saves possible hurt due to ambiguity. A contract should cover such routine things as frequency and length of sessions, whether homework assignments are to be required and the need to bring the completed assignments to the sessions. How available will the counsellor be to the client? Are you happy for the client to telephone you when in need? Remember that this may mean calls late at night or at inconvenient times. Just how available will you be?

THE PURPOSE OF THE COUNSELLING. This should be implicit in the model and approach to counselling which is being used, but it is often helpful to be fairly explicit. For example you may agree that this counselling relationship exists to overcome an immediate crisis. Or it may be to help mend a broken relationship. Or more usually it is to tackle a particular problem through an exploration of the underlying causes which the counsellor will explore with the consent and co-operation of the client. However, integrity demands that we also state (to those who could be expected to comprehend) that we believe the issue being addressed is merely a part of God's overall plan in conforming the client to the image of Christ. Failure to do so could cast God in the role of 'problem solver' and we have already alluded to the fact that there is more evidence that God uses life's problems and difficulties, than there is that he solves them in a painless and miraculous way.

KEEPING RECORDS. It is always recommended that the counsellor keeps records. The old proverb, 'the weakest ink is stronger than the strongest memory' becomes increasingly apparent with the passing of years and increasing case load. There are counselling ministries that claim they never take notes in a counselling session out of deference to the counsellee. However, it is the experience of most counsellors that less than one percent of counsellees are ever bothered by the process of note taking. In fact the opposite is more likely to be the case, they believe they are being taken seriously. When there is any doubt a statement such as: 'I hope you don't mind my taking a few notes, but my mind is like a sieve and what you are saying is far too important to risk me forgetting.' There will, of course be times when you will want to put down the pad and just 'live through' the story with the client and quickly make some notes after they have gone. Actually it's always a good thing to take a few moments after the session to ensure you have recorded all the pertinent facts.

Remember that legally the client is now able to see all records made about them. Never write anything which is not based on fact or information given by the client. Your personal observations should always be written in a form in which you would not mind them being seen by the client.

HOMEWORK It is particularly important that the exact instructions for any homework assignments are recorded on your notes as well. Then to further ensure against heartache, be sure the counsellee writes down the instructions as well or write them down for him or her in much the same way as a doctor would write out a prescription.

ENSURE CONFIDENTIALITY at all times. The guidelines for confidentiality should be included in any statement of ethics. The guidelines given by the Association of Christian Counsellors are an excellent summary of the issues of confidentiality and should be followed at all times.

ARE YOU A VOLUNTEER OR A PROFESSIONAL? What training have you undertaken and how much have you invested in the ministry of counselling? Do you need to meet your expenses in order to carry on, or do you need to be paid a fair rate for the work you are undertaking? Can you afford undertaking this ministry as a form of giving to people? If you do need to be compensated you need to be unashamedly up front about your fees, if you don't but would welcome donations to the ministry you represent - say so. Please analyse your reasons for charging fees and be absolutely positive that your motivation is not just to be 'professional'. We have the uneasy feeling that this is sometimes a major motivating factor. If you charge for counselling, your fees should also be agreed before the counselling begins and should be stated in any contract.

ENDING THE COUNSELLING RELATIONSHIP. Strike a balance between the two extremes of, on the one hand being committed to seeing the problem through to its conclusion and, on the other, developing an un-healthy, on-going relationship which can develop into co-dependency. Do not be afraid to end a series of contacts if less than satisfactory progress is being made. It is often helpful to have a break from each other, and in a few months time the client may be much more able and willing to take matters further.

AVOIDING CO-DEPENDENCY. The term co-dependency is not limited to members of a family who live with an addicted person. It may also be used to describe compulsive people-helpers (people-rescuers) with an unhealthy need to be needed. As counsellors we need to check our own motives, because if we are motivated by a need to be needed we may stifle the person's recovery and even manipulate them to perpetuate their problem so that they still need our help. There is a fine line that exists between the condition of co-dependency and the loving care and support to which God calls us. By maintaining a close relationship with God, and by having an adequate sense of God's calling, we can rest in a safe place and so be free from any harmful dependency. Our identity should be found in who we are in Christ, not the title 'counsellor'.

3. THE FIRST CONTACT WITH THE CLIENT

First impressions are important, and the first one or two contacts will set the tone for future work. Counsellors must learn to share themselves effectively and appropriately in the early counselling sessions.

INTRODUCTION TO THE COUNSELLING SESSION. It is vital that the first session starts in a welcoming and accepting way. Remember that you are on home territory, and the client will be at best nervous, and quite possibly terrified. Make sure they are comfortable and feel secure. There should be no interruptions, no telephones and no unexpected intrusions.

EXPLAIN THE COUNSELLING PROCESS. Do not assume that the client instinctively knows what will happen. If necessary discuss the counselling contract, but it is usually preferable to give it to the client in writing and invite questions either straightaway or at a later date. Deal in a sensitive manner with any questions or anxieties which the client has.

SHOULD YOU START WITH PRAYER? It could, occasionally, be inappropriate to start the first session off with prayer . A disillusionment with God and religious activities may well be one of the problem areas of the client. However, having said this, opening with prayer is a declaration of our dependence on God and of the Holy Spirit being *the* Counsellor. Prayer makes a statement that we are expecting at least some level of supernatural involvement. The testimony of opening in prayer actually establishes the authority by which the counsellor can go beyond merely helping clients identify their emotions and possible contributing factors - the counsellor can dare to give direction in living as well. Obviously, this is an awesome responsibility, but the act of prayer reminds both parties that this direction cannot be the counsellor's opinion, but sound counsel based on God's wisdom.

RELIGIOUS? When counselling a non-Christian opening with prayer could erect barriers. Many have been 'vaccinated' against Christianity by religious practices which, to them, represent a pharisaical type of piety. It could even be considered unethical in that it imposes a 'religious' ethos on the session. Therefore, any attempts at opening or closing in prayer must above all project a genuineness of heart <u>without the slightest hint of Christian jargon</u>. (There will be more specific content on this in the next chapter.) People operating in such conditions will need to adapt the contents of this chapter to accommodate their mission.   .

CONTENT OF THE FIRST SESSION. In the first one or two sessions the suggested content could therefore include:

> Making the client feel safe and comfortable.
> Explaining the counselling methods and processes that may be used.
> Discussing the programme, timing and commitment needed.
> Laying the foundations for a trusting relationship.
> Beginning with the client's life story.
> Initial exploration of their attitudes and beliefs.
> First introduction to the problems as they perceive them.

CLOSING THE SESSION. In closing the session it is usually helpful to end in prayer (if appropriate). It is polite to ask the counsellee if they are comfortable with this and to ask them if they would be willing to close in prayer themselves. This has an added bonus in that they usually recap the counselling session and reiterate the steps that need to be taken, re-enforcing your efforts. In marriage counselling the one closing in prayer is making a declaration of intent in front of their spouse which may be an even more powerful dynamic. Prayer should not be forced onto people, and any prayers said should be simple, straightforward and honest conversations with the Father. The ideal is for the counsellor to finally pray for protection for the client, and that they will continue to deal with the issues raised during the session in the ensuing days.

4. *FORMING AND BUILDING RELATIONSHIPS*

The three activities which the counsellor needs to concentrate on in the early stages are showing acceptance, exhibiting genuineness and giving encouragement. In addition the counsellor should learn how to share out of their own life experience when it is appropriate.

ACCEPTANCE. We should accept all people as equal and valuable in the sight of God. Thus we need to work on our own feelings in order that we come into line with God on this point. We don't need to accept sin and bad behaviour, but we must learn to love all people as Jesus did.

WARMTH AND GENUINENESS. We need a genuine joy in discovering about other people, wanting to share in some of their life's experiences.

ENCOURAGEMENT. To be an encourager involves a degree of sharing and involvement with people, not just with our words, but by our belief that God wishes to encourage and comfort all of us, no matter how sinful or broken we are.

SHARING YOURSELF. The counsellor should bear in mind three questions:-

1. How can I share myself in a way that doesn't sound like a CV, but does open up the way for the client to respond in sharing

2. Who are you? We must encourage the clients to share honestly about themselves.

3. How do I build trust? How do I create a relationship with the client which is based on trust which can therefore act as a bridge across which information will be carried in both directions? Time spent in developing this relationship is never wasted so long as the efforts are invested wisely.

When you build bridges, there are many stages in the trust-building process. Polite chit-chat will only carry the process so far, but early intimate probing could be tantamount to building without a solid foundation. We would like to suggest a few stages, but to make it clear that the exact order will vary because of the human factor.

Some tips and suggestions on the process of sharing will include:

Avoid cliche ridden chit-chat. Make a commitment to avoid topics like the weather or politics. Always concentrate on the life, thoughts and opinions of the person in front of you. (Gardening, DIY or having to replace a major piece of furniture are topics which touch on taste, finances and changing times.). While we all tend to start relationships with cliches, make an effort to quickly move on to the person who is before you, and begin to listen to their views and opinions.

Look for common ground between you. These can include sports, hobbies, background and experiences and church affiliation.

Use open ended questions to discover about the client's life, work and social environment. Use such questions as - 'Tell me about your home and family'; 'How do you spend a normal day?'; 'What upsets you most in your daily life?' It is a good training exercise to practice asking open ended questions to get the client talking. Everyone (with very few exceptions) likes to talk about themselves, they just need the opportunity and a listening ear and they will be away.

Exchanging testimonies is often helpful with Christian clients. Briefly tell how you came to Christ and ask how they did. If their testimony is uncertain or deficient then note this for future exploration. It is not conducive to a counselling relationship if you immediately pounce on the person and ask them if they are really 'born-again'. Some counsellors like to keep 'Knowing God Personally' tracts on hand to give to people who seem uncertain about their salvation.[1]

Acknowledge the person's doubts and uncertainties without passing judgement. A book which may be of value when a person has serious doubts is *Disappointment with God* by Philip Yancey.[2]

Lastly, we need to assess the intellectual, emotional and spiritual needs of the client within this relationship. Some Christians prefer a more cerebral approach to their problems whilst others prefer a more 'celestial' one. The latter will require a more overtly spiritual approach - one that the more cerebral might view as simplistic. Both can be equally valid as long as we recognise that all problems require a balance between the personal involvement of the client and the working of the Holy Spirit. It is a matter of being all things to all people.[3]

5. *LISTENING AND QUESTIONING*

Perhaps the most important skill in counselling is the ability to listen to what the client is saying. Listening as used in counselling involves more than just hearing the words spoken by the person. The words need to be married up with the body language and the voice tone, and then interpreted in the light of the life experiences of the person. Thus, the end result of 'listening' is to begin to understand what experiences, ideas and emotions the person is trying to communicate. The ability to encourage the person to talk with appropriate and well-timed questions is an integral part of the listening process.

THE ART OF LISTENING:

implies concentration, so that many people find that half an hour is as much as they can manage at one session.

involves listening to the hidden words. Many people do not finish sentences and assume the words have been said. Also people will use alternate words to try to avoid using certain words which they find painful. If the client keeps talking about 'she', you may have to gently ask which 'she' she is talking about!

requires the observation of the body language used by the client. Most of us find that words are inadequate to convey our true feelings, but our body language enlarges on the words used. Of course sometimes the words being used and the body language seem to contradict each other. In such circumstances we tend to believe the body language rather than the words.

also opens up the feelings of the person and allows them to communicate in a non-threatening way. People like to be listened to - often they will say that no-one ever listens to them - and they well may be right in this. So the counsellor, by listening, honours the person and encourages them to share deeper and more personal feelings. This is the aim of the listening process, not so much to hear the story, but rather to share the feelings that the person felt as they lived that story.

QUESTIONING

The ability to ask good and appropriate questions is vital for a counsellor. Good questioning facilitates openness if the questions are appropriate, timely and asked in an encouraging way. Exactly the same question - for example - 'How did you get on with your father' - can either open up the way to deeper communication, or shut the person up completely. The counsellor has to learn how to ask questions, when to ask them, and also discern when the person is ready to answer them. All of this takes experience, but the principles are fairly straight forward.

Ask open-ended questions rather than closed ones. The best questions are the ones which require the client to think, to develop and to explore. Closed questions are easily answered and usually only involve thinking rather than feeling. Open ended questions seek to open up the feelings of the person as well as their thoughts and memories.

After asking your open question, give the person time to think and answer before asking another question. The best open-ended question may result in a period of silence before the person answers. Be patient, encourage and listen to the whole person.

Avoiding leading questions. The question needs to be 'neutral' so that the person can answer either way. So, for example, don't ask 'You really didn't like your mother, did you?', but rather ask 'How did you really get on with your mother?'

Don't keep pressing with questions if the client seems unwilling to answer fully - it may not be the right time. Make a note that a full answer was avoided; it may be possible to come back to it. The same question asked at a later stage may be answered in a completely different way. You need to discern where the client is, and if an exploratory question is rebuffed, store it away for future use and take a different tack.

Often if a question is 'on target' clients will struggle to answer, perhaps with their emotions coming to the surface as they form the words. At this time the wise counsellor may choose to relieve the tension appropriately by such techniques as - stopping for a cup of tea, which gives the client time to think, or by the counsellor saying a few words about his or her own reactions. For example you could say something like: 'If that had happened to me I would have felt gutted.' Sometimes it may be wise to stop a particular flow and change direction, making a note to come back to the painful area on a future occasion. We may well forget that our clients are very vulnerable, confused and often scared of what there is to be found. The good counsellor is gentle, loving and considerate in the early stages when the client is beginning to share who they are and the problems they have.

Ask the questions in a tone of voice and with a body language which shows that you are genuinely interested in the answer.

And finally - when you have asked a question, make sure you listen to the answer!

A MODEL OF COMMUNICATION

We all have different personalities, and due to our upbringing we tend to communicate in quite different ways. Some people can 'exteriorise' or share their feelings much better than other people. Some people have developed a way of speaking which conveys messages effectively. Many of us find that, despite ourselves, other people perceive messages which we didn't intend sending. We often forget that the words we use in conversation are themselves translations of the thoughts we have. Bilingual people find that they 'think' in one language but can then translate the words into the other language automatically. The language in which we think is very personal. No one else shares exactly the same vocabulary as you do. No one else thinks in the same way as you do. Your thoughts and feelings are unique and a part of your personality. Words *never* convey the whole truth.

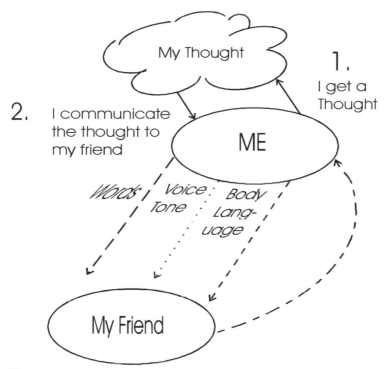

3. My Friend then has to respond to the thought using the same process.

Much work has been done on the way we use our voices and bodies to complete the message of the words. Many researchers say that when we communicate only about 15% of the message is in the words used. About 30% of the meaning is in the tone of voice, and the remaining 55% of the message is in the body language. Perhaps that is why I (Mike) hate telephones, as I am never sure what the person at the other end of the line is really thinking. I much prefer face-to-face communication so I can 'see' what the person is really saying.

When the person we are communicating with 'hears' our message, they also have to translate it into their own mind's language.

We often forget that words such as 'home' can mean something completely different to another person. We have to be careful not to assume that the other person has fully understood what we have said. We have to wait until the feedback loop is closed and the reaction and answers we receive back are understood, and until agreement has been reached between the two parties as to the content of the message being communicated.

This counselling skill of giving feedback is much neglected, but is very important for 'peeling back the layers of the onion' and going to deeper levels of understanding at subsequent counselling sessions.

6.   GAINING INSIGHT AND UNDERSTANDING

As the counselling process progresses, the counsellor will be asking the following questions. Do I understand what is going on in this person's life? Can I distinguish between the problems initially presented by the client and the hidden issues, often lying below the surface, which have fed those problems and caused them to become an issue at this time?

Gaining insight and understanding into people is one skill which can't really be taught. It involves the mature disciplines of perception, reflection and integration of information. It takes wisdom to know what to ask, and sometimes boldness to challenge the client to go deeper and face issues which may be repressed because of pain or shame.

The whole process requires a cycle of enquiry which may need to be repeated several times as new aspects of the problem emerge, and the client has the time and space to reflect on the counsellor's insights.

THIS *CYCLE OF UNDERSTANDING* CONSISTS OF:

Ask a suitable question - encourage and enable the person to answer - listen and observe -'hear' what is said - reflect on the meaning - feedback this meaning to the client - hear their response - clarify the meaning of the answer - integrate into your understanding - then finally begin the cycle again by asking the next question.

One of the greatest failings I have observed in doctors and counsellors is failing to 'hear' what people say. In my early days I (Mike) would tape-record consultations, and was horrified just how many times I would ask a question, but then not listen to the reply before I launched into another question. This is a skill which must be practised - to ask a question, then relax, not thinking of the next question you will ask, but instead concentrating on the answer, clarifying what is being said, and letting the answer naturally lead on to more questions.

TAKING A 'HISTORY'

It was stated earlier that people don't want to hear our answers until they are sure we understand the problem, and indeed we shouldn't start giving answers until we do adequately understand the problem. Unfortunately, most of us have a tendency to overestimate our grasp of a problem. Generally speaking the more in depth information there is available, then the clearer the counsellor's perspective will be. What does it mean to take a history? Well, it means to delve into, examine, explore, inquire, question, peruse, probe and search in the most gentle and sensitive way possible. A good history not only identifies problem trends and repeated events, but the person's strengths as well. A certain amount of information can also be gained through information gathering homework assignments in the form of questionnaires, lists and logging of activities. Good information, properly assessed, is a necessary ingredient in developing a successful strategy for future sessions. CWR's 10 points is one example of a good starting framework, but any such 'checklist' is only a generality which is followed up through sensitivity to the Holy Spirit. Above all avoid making the client feel they are being 'cross examined' by a prosecuting attorney.

7. ASSESSMENT OF PEOPLE

During this phase of getting to understand the problems we also need to understand the people themselves. We all have different personalities and experiences and these will affect how we see and react to stressful situations. It may be worth spending some time completing simple personality tests (such as the commonly used Myers-Briggs Type Indicator), which can help both the counsellor and the client to understand why the person reacts in certain ways.[4] This topic is covered in more detail in a later chapter.

We need to recognise that past events, and even past counselling, may have affected the person. The more we know about them, the more we are likely to understand all the 'whys' in their life. In this respect we also need to assess the spiritual perception of the client, and sensitively enquire as to previous religious experiences, especially where these have been hurtful. Just asking the question, 'Have you been upset or hurt by previous ministry, prayer or counselling?' can be quite illuminating.

We also need to recognise the effect of culture on the beliefs and attitudes of the client. Culture consists of all the beliefs and environmental influences which we experience as we grow up. Clearly if the person grew up in an African village their culture will be quite foreign to our own. However, we should also remember that even with people born and reared in this country, their cultural upbringing and experiences may have been completely different to our own.

Look at the person's strengths and weaknesses. It is well worth while concentrating for a whole session on the good points in a person. So often we are criticised and dragged down by others. But everyone has strengths, and concentrating on these is always productive. Devise a series of questions and activities which enable people to describe and demonstrate their good points. Encourage them and build them up in this way.

8. BUILDING A DEEPER LEVEL OF UNDERSTANDING OF A PERSON AND THEIR PROBLEMS

To summarise this process of truly understanding both the people and the problems they present, we need to focus on the following questions. (They are offered, not as questions to actually ask, but rather as a mental checklist to help us make sure that the ground has been adequately covered.)

PRESENTING PROBLEMS
What is actually happening in this person?
What are his or her problems?
How have things progressed to the present state?
What situation is she or he in? What difficulties does he or she face?
What are his or her feelings?

133

BACKGROUND TO THEIR PROBLEMS

What is the history to how these problems have developed?

What are the recent events which have precipitated these problems?

What previous events have had an influence on the present situation?

What are the person's perceptions, beliefs and attitudes?

What cultural issues affect the problems?

What sort of childhood and upbringing did the client have?

Is the client in paid employment?

How does he or she spend a normal day?

PAST EVENTS

Have they had similar problems in the past?

What illnesses have they had?

What stresses have they been under?

PERSONALITY

How does the person describe himself or herself?

What are his or her weaknesses and strengths?

What are his or her character traits?

How does he or she perceive their situation?

How open is the client? Is he or she being honest?

How much does the client trust you? How much has been revealed?

RELATIONSHIPS

What is the client's relationship with the rest of his or her family like?

Does he or she have a supporting group of friends?

Does he or she have a confidant with whom problems can be shared?

INSIGHT AND UNDERSTANDING

How much insight does the person have?

How strong is his or her will?

What does the client see as his or her problems?

SPIRITUAL HISTORY

What has been the client's Christian experience?

Does he or she see themselves as committed Christians?

Is he or she in Christian fellowship?

What experience has the client had of prayer and ministry?

What painful religious memories does he or she have?

What is the client's understanding of the work of the Holy Spirit within us?

ACTIONS TAKEN

What actions have the client taken to try to help?

Has other professional help been sought?

Has the client developed trusting relationships with others?

As you write up your notes you can then begin to fill out these sections, gaining a fuller insight into the person and the problems they have.

9. PRACTICE MAKES PERFECT

All the gifts of counselling - both human skills and God's spiritual gifts - need to be exercised to perfect them. All of the counselling skills need developing and applying in a learning environment. Please avoid the arrogance of believing that God's gifts are perfect and therefore do not need to be developed. Whether it is preaching, or even something as supernatural as healing, we believe we need to grow in using God's gifts under the guidance of a mature teacher. The 'amateur' Christian minister can do harm as well as good. This normally occurs when the person interposes their own beliefs and personality onto the gift which God is giving so distorting or stunting the ability or gift.

In a later chapter we include a series of exercises which help to develop counselling skills. These should be practised, preferably in groups of three, throughout the training period.

This chapter has concentrated on the basic counselling skills and so far we haven't talked much about therapy or helping the person. However, we need to recognise just how therapeutic it is for people to be listened to, to be understood, to be encouraged, and to be given the space to reflect on who they are, and what their problems really are. Often that is all the therapy a person will need. In the next chapter we will concentrate on the skills of therapy which are characteristic of Christian counselling models. But remember, a good counsellor will often hear the words, 'Thank you for listening to me. No one else has really done that. It has been a great comfort. I feel better already.'

END OF CHAPTER NOTES

1. 'Knowing God Personally' tracts available from Agape (formerly Campus Crusade for Christ), Fairgate House, Kings Road, Tyseley, Birmingham B11 2AA

2. *Disappointment with God* by Philip Yancey published by Zondervan, Michigan in 1988

3. 1 Corinthians 9: 22

4. A useful book is *Naturally Gifted* by Gordon and Rosemary Jones, published by Scripture Union, London 1991

FURTHER SKILLS IN CHRISTIAN COUNSELLING

In this chapter we outline the specific skills needed by the Christian counsellor. No one counsellor will be an expert in all of these skills, but they paint a picture of the range of skills required. One of the key skills required of the counsellor is that of **knowing your own limitations.** Knowing when to refer on to another counsellor or doctor is essential to avoid getting out of your depth and causing harm to the client, either through errors of commission or of omission.

This is a very brief resume of counselling skills, and each model of Christian counselling will stress some skills and emphasise different aspects and techniques. We suggest that the skills outlined in this chapter will form a firm foundation on which you will be able to build the specific skills and knowledge of the counselling model (or models) which you will use in ministry.

The main skills of helping people through Christian models of counselling include:-

1 Facilitating the client's disclosure - through encouragement, body language, prompting, sharing and empathy.

2 Understanding the complexity of problems presented understanding the effects of inheritance, culture, upbringing, and

the spiritual climate during the client's early years.

3 Agreeing these problems with the client - helping people to have discernment, agreeing with God over the problem, providing comfort and challenge as appropriate.

4 Counselling God's truth and wisdom - using the Bible appropriately and effectively, knowing how to gently challenge and confront, and handle moral absolutes.

5 Giving hope - that change will come, understanding God's time-scale.

6 Leading the person towards a closer relationship with God.

7 Being a channel for the Holy Spirit - praying with people, using the spiritual gifts and deliverance.

1. FACILITATING THE CLIENT'S DISCLOSURE

The counsellor first needs to provide the client with a suitable environment and space in which to facilitate the sharing of issues. This will then allow clients to express their thoughts, feelings, doubts and fears.

The Christian counsellor encourages and facilitates clients as discussed in the previous chapter with the following additional skills:-

Using correct prompting through both natural questions and supernatural ones. Often God may put things into your mind during the counselling process, a sensitive and timely question along these lines may be the key to opening up the problem. However a word of caution - *never* say - 'God has told me that ...' Just bring the question in naturally, not necessarily indicating that God has suggested it, unless this will encourage and support the client's own revelations.

Use a sensitive and timely sharing of yourself, your testimony and your faith in God. This should not be used to 'preach' to the client, but rather facilitate their own sharing.

Show empathy as indicated by a willingness to see things from their point of view. Clients need to know that you really care. That you are more than objective and professional but also a fellow traveller through life's difficulties.

2. UNDERSTANDING THE COMPLEXITY OF PROBLEMS PRESENTED

The good counsellor has an open and enquiring mind and wants to find an answer to questions like these: 'What has happened in this person's life? How has he or she reacted to these events? What effects have these events had?' Many things influence us and play a part in making us unique individuals. The counsellor needs to keep all of the following aspects in mind when building up a picture of who the person is, and what has happened to him or her.

INHERITANCE: We are all influenced greatly by the inheritance we receive when we are born. It is generally accepted that approximately half of our physical, mental and emotional characteristics are given to us before birth. We understand that our genes decide our physical make-up, but what gives us our mental and emotional personality? Many attributes are clearly passed down in families, although it is difficult at times to distinguish between the inherited aspects and the influence parents have over their children. It is not uncommon for mental illness such as depression to run through several generations. Is this genetic, or due to upbringing? Whatever the scientists eventually decide, there is no disagreement that taking full details of the client's family history and any previous traumatic events within the extended family, is a vital first step to placing a person within the context in which they were developed.

The circumstances and influences which build on this inheritance are Culture, Environment, Upbringing, Life Events and possibly Abuse.

CULTURE: We often forget the importance of culture in our development. Culture influences our life patterns, belief systems and perspective on the world around us. Later on in life we may not like or agree with the cultural norms, but they are so ingrained within us that we find it very difficult to go against our early patterns of behaviour. Obviously if someone is raised in a foreign country we expect them to have different beliefs and customs. But culture also varies considerably within our own country. For example, we all have a spiritual culture which will be influenced by the churches we attended as we were growing up.

ENVIRONMENT: Poverty, arguing parents and painful events are all part of our environment and can have a marked effect on the young. A sudden death accompanied by open grief within the family will leave its mark on the majority of children. However young the child is, he or she will pick up the 'vibrations' around them. In my early days as a country GP, I (Mike) was amazed at the number of calls for visits which I would receive at around 9.00 p.m. The typical story was of a young mother who had had a crying baby all day. She had tried all known methods to calm the child but it was still crying. Could I come out now to save a visit in the middle of the night? The journey to the house usually took around half an hour and invariably I was greeted at the door by a sheepish looking mother who explained that the child was now fast asleep. Whatever had started off the crying, the tension in the mother had played a part in keeping it going. As soon as mother relaxed, because the doctor was coming, the baby could breathe a sigh of relief and fall asleep.

UPBRINGING: Children so often become like their parents, even when they hated their parents and vowed to never be like them. Parents are such a powerful role model that lifelong influences occur without conscious thought or effort. As there are no perfect parents, the potential for harmful influence is great. I (Mike) have a lovely daughter who was adopted by us while a few weeks old. She clearly has a different genetic make-up to us, and in many ways is completely different from my wife and me. However, a father's influence over his daughter is one of the most important factors in the formation of a girl's personality, and now my daughter will often remark that, even against her will, she finds herself reacting in the same way that I did. Fortunately she is strong enough and mature enough to realise what is going on, and is slowly becoming her own woman, although I expect that my 'imprint' on her will always be discernible. Incidentally I believe that my wife has had an equally strong influence (for good!) over our three sons.

Today an increasing number of people come from broken or dysfunctional families. Many children are being reared by one parent, or even by two adults of the same sex. There is increasing evidence to show that all other possible arrangements are not as healthy as a secure family with father, mother, grandparents and numerous uncles and aunts. However, no one is able to choose their family, so we need to accept people as they are in this respect, and help them to understand what effects their upbringing have had upon them.

LIFE EVENTS: Life consists of one traumatic event after another! It is perfectly healthy for a child to experience the normal human disappointments and difficulties. We should not shield children from death, whether of their pet rabbit or of their favourite grandfather. Disappointment or failure should be the spur to try harder having learned the appropriate lessons. The child has to try and push on all boundaries and restrictions, and sometimes will get hurt. However, we increasingly see that the trauma of some events has overwhelmed the child, and they have not been able to cope with their reaction. A process of repression and denial of hurt is common in such circumstances, and many people will completely repress (and therefore forget) traumatic experiences which were too much for them.

ABUSE: It is also sad to note that many children are severely abused and sinned against in a way in which no child can cope. Abuse may be physical or sexual, but it may also be mental and emotional. Starving a child of love and affection is probably as bad as (if not worse than) beating them. It is of course hardest when the abuse has come from a close family member. When abused the child can usually only react in one of two ways. Both of these reactions will themselves also produce long term harmful effects in the child. The child may become withdrawn, quiet, fearful of strangers, retreating into their own fantasy world in which hurtful events don't happen. Alternatively the child will rebel against the abuser and become 'naughty', showing disobedience and wilfulness as a defence reaction. This child will almost certainly find itself abusing other weaker children in turn, and this pattern often stays into adult life. The battered child may become a battering parent.

When exploring this area of abuse it is important to note the following principles:

1 Abuse happens to all of us - it is the degree of abuse which varies. Get the clients to speak out not only what happened to them, but how they reacted to it - both what they felt and what they did.

2 Discuss how they coped with the situation. What defence mechanisms did they develop, and how do these operate today. For example if the reaction was to withdraw and deny, are they still doing the same today?

3 Feelings about events will come out when talking, but may deepen and become distressing if the counsellor really probes too deeply and too quickly. A degree of comfort and reassurance about the abuse is usually needed before deeper exploration can take place.

4 Only when the nature of the sin committed against the client is fully acknowledged can healing begin to take place through the giving of forgiveness.

5 Almost certainly the abused person will feel guilt, often translated into the belief that he or she in some way deserved the abuse. A gentle encouragement to understand that any power or domination over a child is actually evil, will help the client see that the abuser, as a sinner like ourselves, needs

help and forgiveness.

6 The process of truly forgiving someone who has hurt us deeply is a lengthy process to which the client and counsellor will usually need to return on several occasions.

7 Asking God to give a 'spirit of repentance' into the situation and seeking to pray for the abuser may be a turning point in the therapy.

8 Clients often need to also ask forgiveness for themselves, recognising their own reaction to the abuse. A prayer of forgiveness, cleansing and healing is usually required.

PERSONALITY DEVELOPMENT: It is again obvious to say that everyone's personality is unique, but research has demonstrated that there are very similar patterns in most people. As we have described elsewhere you can describe a personality profile which describes much of how a person will react and behave in certain situations. Our behaviour patterns depend on a multitude of factors including our upbringing and our personalities. These are mainly unconsciously learned behaviours. To correct unsuitable patterns of behaviour is difficult and requires hard work and application on the part of the client. The Holy Spirit aids us in this work, but God does not replace the effort required, rather He seems to support us in our self-discipline and application.

SELF-AWARENESS: A vital aspect of growth is a correct level of self-awareness. There is nothing worse than a client who steadfastly refuses to see what is staring the counsellor, and others close to them, in the face. In our experience, only God can challenge correctly enabling a person to grow in the development of a correct self-image, and the counsellor has to be aware of what needs to happen and then pray and encourage whilst the change is taking place.

MENTAL HABITS AND ILLNESS: A part of the personality make-up of many people is a tendency towards mental traits of anxiety or depression. Some people are more moody than others, while others find obsessive traits and depressed reactions an inevitable response to difficult situations. The client needs to acknowledge these reactions and seek to correct wrong reactions through the power of the Spirit and Spirit-led practical work.

SPIRITUAL PERCEPTIONS: Christian counselling recognises the importance of the person's spirit in controlling these mental and emotional reactions. Often there have been religious experiences in childhood which have produced a distorted view of God. Many people see God as a strict father who will punish them for their failures. Developing a correct view of God may take up much of the counselling process.

CONSCIENCE AND GUILT: We have all sinned and fallen short of God's ideal for us. Many people see their sins as somehow worse than those of other people. It is not uncommon to find people who believe that they have committed the unpardonable sin. Reassurance needs to be given that anyone coming to God in a repentant attitude will be forgiven. False guilt needs to be examined and exposed, but true guilt resulting from sin can only be dealt with through the actions of repentance and receiving of forgiveness from God.

THE OCCULT: Finally, the occult can have powerful influences on people, either directly through personal involvement, or indirectly through curses spoken over them, or familial curses which may be passed down through the generations. Holy Spirit led prayer, and then taking the actions indicated, will always deal with occult influences, although extended periods of help may be needed with some people. *SEE APPENDIX B.*

3. AGREE ABOUT THE PROBLEMS

Many counsellors feel that they can clearly see the client's problems and get frustrated when the client doesn't see things in the same way. It is only half of the battle for the counsellor to understand what is going on. He or she has to get the client to agree as well, or no change will take place.

The *Mikdav window* described in chapter six reminds us that we should not attempt to challenge the client until they are stable enough to accept that challenge and work with it. Most people need some form of comforting in the early stages of a counselling process. How should this happen?

There are three levels of comforting available to us -

> **SYMPATHY**   Sharing in a person's problems in a sympathetic way is the first and obvious approach. This will give some comfort but does not help the person to face up to the problems they face and so deal with them successfully.

> **EMPATHY**   Entering into the person's shoes and seeing events as they saw them is a help to understand and support the client. However the counsellor needs to keep some objectivity during this process or they too may be dragged down into the problem and so collude with the client.

COMPASSION   Compassion as given by God is the ideal approach to comforting people. This is the approach taken by Jesus in which he indicated real love for the person, but hate towards the sin which was binding them.

God's comfort is the best medicine for our clients. Only he can comfort and protect us at the same time. Only he can lovingly challenge and confront in a way which brings growth and healing. When the client can see his or her problems from God's point of view then the real battle is over.

Having been comforted appropriately by the counsellor, it is important to gently but firmly lead the client between the woolly area of collusion, denial and dependency, and the minefield of mindless challenge in an unstable person, into the fertile land of analysis and action under the authority of the Holy Spirit.

4. COUNSELLING GOD'S TRUTH AND WISDOM

When the client has reached a satisfactory degree of stability, it is important to start the process of counselling God's wisdom and truth into their lives. How do you determine when this point has been reached? A combination of experience, cautious advance and God's timing will be needed. Don't be afraid to try a gentle advance and be prepared to retreat for a while if the client reacts badly to it. Good homework assignments are particularly useful here as the client can tackle issues at their own speed and in their own way. The feedback at the next session will guide the counsellor as to how ready the client is to begin work on their problems.

DEVELOP HOMEWORK ASSIGNMENTS

Christian counselling involves more than identifying problems and telling clients why they exist. It is also helping them apply the truth of scripture to their life. This is accomplished by involving clients in situations that will give them experience at applying a particular principle. Often these situations are created through homework assignments. There are three types of homework assignments - data gathering, wisdom and action, and they fit into various stages of the counselling process.

DATA assignments are research, mainly to give the counsellor insight. These include:

Testing instruments, temperament analyses.

Questionnaires - designed to show the client's history and or habit patterns.

Logs, Lists, Records - designed to find how the client spends his or her time.

Consultations with other specialists - physical examinations.

WISDOM assignments are mainly to give the counsellee insight. This may involve some of the same as above, but the purpose will be to impress the client with certain facts concerning his or her problem. For example:

'Log every time you lose your temper this week. Record the time and circumstances.'

'List 50 areas where you have failed as a husband.'

'Record the way you use your time on a chart that divides the day into 15-minute blocks.'

'List 50 positive qualities about your spouse.'

'List 50 ways to demonstrate love to your spouse.'

Bible studies are wisdom assignments and can be done in several ways:

'Meditate on one of these Scripture texts each day and record what they say to you.'

'Read the book of Proverbs and list all the verses dealing with anger.'

'Read Romans 8:28 and Proverb 16:4 and 21:1. Write a paragraph on why they are similar and a possible application to your situation.'

Alternatively the counsellor can choose a passage which covers the truth in question and prepare questions which will draw the client to the obvious conclusion:

Considering Matthew 18:21-35, 'Why did the Lord tell this story with such absurd contrasts in debts?'

'What does this parable tell us about the consequences of unforgiveness?'

Christian books and tapes on specific topics also prove useful wisdom assignments. Asking clients to write a report on a book or a selected chapter helps to crystallise thoughts.

ACTION Since Christian counselling involves a process of putting off the old and putting on the new, behaviour homework assignments will help bring this change about and reinforce it. Work through the following stages with the client:

a. Identify the specific un-biblical behaviour to put off.

b. Determine appropriate biblical behaviour to put on.

c. Use this appropriate behaviour as a goal in structuring a concrete assignment. Begin with easier goals which build hope; then move on.

For example (stage C):
> 'Each evening, share with your spouse one aggravation and one blessing from your work day.'
> 'Spend two evenings per week in study for your degree.'
> 'Spend at least ten minutes praying aloud, as a couple, daily.'

Does your client lack discipline? Is he lazy, insensitive or inconsiderate? Wisdom assignments such as a list of ways to demonstrate love will make him aware of how inconsiderate he has been, but assigning him to walk the dog every evening so his wife won't have to, will get him started actually doing something about it. Love is an action word.

5. GIVING HOPE

Giving hope runs simultaneously with building trust. It can be done in many ways, but one thing you can be sure about is that minimising the client's problem is not one of them. People don't want to hear your answer until they are sure you understand the problem. Listen to the full force of what they are saying. Their presentation problem may appear minimal, but chances are there is much more to it. But even if there isn't more, it was still big enough in their eyes to bring them to an 'expert'.

Any suggestion for giving hope can sound 'wooden' when written down in a book, and we can all imagine any of the following suggestions being used inappropriately. They all require sensitivity and creativity. Some, in certain situations, and with the right people, can even be used humorously, in other situations not at all.

One source of hope is to remind them that there is a positive side to a crisis, that God will definitely use it in achieving his goal for their lives - to develop the character of Christ. Use Isaiah 43:18,19 to point out that the past does not have to predict the future.

> Do not remember the former things, Nor consider the things of old. Behold, I will do a new thing, Now it shall spring forth; Shall you not know it? I will even make a road in the wilderness And rivers in the desert.[1]

People can and do change - sometimes they even grow up! We like to use II Peter 1:3-5 and even on through verse 10 to let them know the Bible even promises a complete change in nature and demonstrates how we can begin to assume responsibility for our own future well-being and happiness.

> His divine power has given to us all things that pertain to life and godliness, through the knowledge of Him who called us by glory and virtue, by which have been given to us exceedingly great and precious promises, that through these you may be partakers of the divine nature, having escaped the corruption that is in the world through lust. But also for this very reason, giving all diligence, add to your faith virtue, to virtue knowledge,[2]

This is not promoting Utopia or independence, but it is encouraging a godly self-control and individual responsibility which in the long term provides much more hope than if they believed they were 'victims' of circumstances.

6. LEADING THE PERSON CLOSER TO GOD

We all need to come closer to God, whatever stage we have

reached in our Christian life. The goal of the counselling process is to do just that! We first need to ascertain how the client's relationship with God has developed, and where the sticking points are.

At times we will need to ask the question, 'Is the person actually a believer?' We have all had different salvation experiences, some in an instant and others taking several years. Some people will testify that for as long as they can remember they have loved and trusted God. However, there are two groups of people with Christian backgrounds who may not have made a personal commitment to Jesus as Lord even though they have been in a Christian environment for many years.

Many people are **Nominal Christians**. They have accepted the existence of God and often practise Christian behaviour, but have never had a real experience of the living God in their lives. Gentle enquiry may reveal that they doubt whether Jesus is a personal saviour to them. The counsellor should be prepared to explain the process of submitting to Jesus.

Others may be described as **Familial Christians** where they have automatically accepted the faith and behaviour of their parents from an early age, but not found a strong personal faith for themselves. Such people will know many of the facts of Christianity, but it never seems to come to life for them. There may well have been a period of backsliding in their youth, and some degree of confusion will exist as to whether they are really Christians or not. Again leading them into a personal relationship with the living God is an important step in their growth process.

7.   BEING A CHANNEL FOR THE HOLY SPIRIT

The most important requirement for a Christian counsellor is the ability to act as a channel for the Holy Spirit to come into people's lives. Most clients have some blockages to God speaking and acting in their lives, and the counsellor comes alongside to pray with the person and through their faith to allow the Holy Spirit to break through the blockages and bring healing. In this respect counselling is like all other Christian ministry.

Counselling is a Holy Spirit led activity, so must be accompanied by intercession and the exercise of faith on the part of the counsellor. Counselling is about change, but not just change on the surface, and not just change in behaviour, but rather change within the heart. This change can only come about through the actions of our spirits in communion with the Holy Spirit. At the heart of counselling is the action of the Holy Spirit in the deepest parts of our hearts. This change needs power, and that power can only come from God. All of us can try hard to change, and of course it is important that we are involved sincerely in any process of change. But the spiritual power can only come from God.

How does the Holy Spirit work? That is a question which would fill several books. We will attempt to sum up how the Holy Spirit seems to work within the counselling model.

The Spirit works in hidden and mysterious ways, and He is always surprising us. We work with the Spirit, but we cannot give him orders, nor can we speak out our wants in prayer, add 'in the name of Jesus' after our prayer, and then expect him to deliver. God wants to work individually with us, and what is right for one person may be quite wrong for another.

Having said that the Spirit works in differing ways, yet there are clear hallmarks following the work of the Spirit. These include a sense of peace, a desire for repentance and restitution following conviction of sin, an increased love of God expressed in deeper levels of worship and increased hunger for his word.

In some people the Spirit works in spectacular ways. Miracles do happen, although not as often as we would wish. Deep problems can be dealt with rapidly and despair turned to joy overnight. However, we should always remember that these wonderful signs are not the end of the affair. Rather they mark the beginning, as the person who has been blessed needs to work through many issues with God. Self-discipline needs to be exercised. The person needs to grow in humility as he or she seeks to take God's blessing and also bless others. We have both seen people who had 'miraculous healing', only to see the person worse off than before after a few weeks had passed.

Many testify to being rendered unconscious by the Holy Spirit who then performs some deep surgery within, resulting in significant change. This we would not dispute. However, there is considerable evidence, both biblically and through observation, that the Holy Spirit's preferred method is to work with a conscious person endeavouring to use all their faculties to understand and co-operate with God's work.

The Spirit seeks to work through us to bless others. The whole purpose of the gifts of the Holy Spirit is so that the Body of Christ may be healed and strengthened to go out to minister to others. It is right to 'earnestly seek the gifts' in order that others may benefit.

In counselling there are three spiritual gifts which should be sought above all others:-

The gift of **KNOWLEDGE** - the word of knowledge guides us as we seek to understand the problems in the client, and then helps us to bring wholeness through God's directions.

The gift of **WISDOM** - is vital to know how and when to use the other gifts to maximum effect. Often there is more wisdom in using spiritual insights to fuel intercession than to speak a prophecy.

The gift of **FAITH** - allows us to pray, challenge and offer wisdom in the knowledge that God will answer our prayer and come and meet the person. In numerous counselling sessions we have felt inadequate and rather foolish. 'What on earth do I do now?' is a frequent cry. But we press on because we have faith that God is in the business of healing.

8.   THE PLACE OF PRAYER IN THE COUNSELLING PROCESS

First let us look at some principles and process concerning praying with non-Christians in the counselling situation. Great tact and consideration is needed, and you must make sure that the person genuinely wishes you to pray for them, and understands that this is not a religious routine, but a genuine talking to God about the situation.

SUGGESTED PROCEDURE FOR PRAYING WITH NON-CHRISTIANS

Always explain, in non-religious terms, what you are going to do. This is hard for most of us brought up in Christian language, but develop a child-like approach, and see prayer as a natural two-way conversation with a loving parent. Avoid religious jargon.

Do not expect the person to actively 'participate', but encourage them to do so if they wish. It is best if the counsellor takes the initiative, and when confidence is developed, then encourage the client to say a few words themselves.

Before praying say something like: 'I believe that -

God is listening to what we say

God is concerned about you

He is willing to guide us both.'

Inform the client that what you will do is:

speak openly to God
encourage the client to listen (eyes closed if he wants to)
then keep silent for a short period.
Tell the client that during this silent time they can reflect on what has been said. Afterwards, he or she may wish to talk about it.

Then pray in the following manner:

a) God our Father (use Lord's prayer type of format)
b) Thank you for listening
for being aware of our deepest needs

for knowing all about our problems
for being concerned.
c) Help us to understand. Give us new insights into our problems.
d) Mention specific issues.

Have a time of silence.

Listen, listen, listen.

Discuss what has happened (in a non-threatening way).

a) Did any thoughts come into your mind?

b) Some of the things I felt or thought are ...

c) What do you think?

Offer up thoughts to God in a closing prayer.

Bless the person.

SUGGESTED PROCEDURE FOR PRAYING WITH CHRISTIANS

When praying for Christians many of the above suggestions are also valid. Many Christians coming for counsel have some degree of unbelief and disappointment with prayer. They may feel obliged to go through with it, but they may not have the faith that God will hear and answer. It is important to understand that, in the beginning, it is the faith of the counsellor which is operating, although the fervent prayer of the counsellor will be that the client's faith will also grow and that they will eventually fully participate in the prayer.

Some specific suggestions when praying with Christians:

Use a similar format to non-Christians, but be more explicit, and perhaps use more Christian expressions in the prayers.

Encourage them to listen to God for themselves during the prayer - remembering that this is almost certainly one of the problems they have. So many clients will say that God doesn't speak to them any more.

Be simple and straightforward, there are no extra marks for lengthy prayers full of the correct Christian jargon. Try to emulate the prayers of Jesus - very short and straight to the point.

Do not impose your own thoughts, feelings, and beliefs onto the person. Recognise that there are many approaches to prayer and the client will need to be confident in the one they use themselves.

Rely on the Holy Spirit during the prayers and expect to receive 'words', impressions and scriptures which may help the counselling process. Encourage the client in whatever they feel or hear themselves.

Try to get them to share what they think God is saying first, but don't show disappointment if they say they heard nothing.

Always be tentative in making suggestions yourself, and obviously, avoiding terms like 'God has told me that ...'

Encourage them to pray for themselves and then write down what they think God is saying.

Explain that you will do the same after the counselling session.

At the next session encourage the client to share what he has experienced in the ensuing period.

Above all keep faith yourself that God is in the business of answering prayers - it's just that he usually chooses some funny ways of answering at times. It is our experience that God is always choosing new and exciting ways of revealing himself to people - so relax and enjoy the experience of working with Almighty God!

CHAPTER END NOTES

1. Isaiah 43:18-19

2. 2 Peter 1:3-5

PEOPLE ARE UNIQUE

Because there are so many factors which contribute to our individuality, it is little wonder that each human being is well and truly unique. In each one of us there are many predictable responses (such as reaction to pain), most of which we share with others, so that to respond in any other way would be unusual and suggest some abnormality. However, once we get beyond these very basic human reactions, the pattern starts to become complex, in fact extremely complex.

Human behaviour, and the attitudes and beliefs which control it, owe much to the way we perceive life and the world around us. Put in its most simple form, we believe there are three basic factors (or groupings of factors) which are widely accepted as forming the main influence on this perception. They are the environment in which we are brought up, our genetic inheritance and our gender (which we humorously refer to as the *EGG* factor) .

ENVIRONMENT, in this instance, covers our entire history of life experiences including those influences mentioned in the last chapter: culture, upbringing and life events. No wonder we are different, as no two people can have exactly the same life experiences.

GENETICS have a lot in common with the *inheritance* discussed in the last chapter. Psychological attempts at quantifying personality seem, predominantly, to be concerned with temperament, which many believe has a strong hereditary component (although most would admit that circumstances, experiences and individual choice have a lot to do with the direction in which these basic traits develop).

Although we are all unique, most of us fit fairly well into certain categories (or possibly a combination of categories), and this is often helpful in understanding human interaction. Previous societies developed such classical characteristic tags as choleric, melancholic, phlegmatic, and sanguine. Some attempts have been made to develop this into a system, however, no proper measuring instruments were ever developed. Personalities are far too complex for most people to feel comfortable just being labelled choleric or sanguine. This same choleric individual may be termed a *Type A* personality when discussing stress, *a High Achiever* in business management, but all of these are simply descriptions of a general category of personality type.

Recently we have seen the development of more sophisticated and scientific methods which use a breakdown of personality functions. These classify and then grade each division of personality, or they identify an individual's preference between extreme possibilities in various areas. These will usually include items such as our tendency to be objective or subjective, or more rigid rather than relaxed. For instance consider the following possible ways of identifying characteristics by asking questions adapted from the Myers-Briggs Type Indicator:

Where do you receive the bulk of your energy? From the outer world or through your inner world?

    Are you energised by your inner world? ***INTROVERT***
    Do you come alive in a crowd? ***EXTROVERT***

How do you obtain information?

    Are you a visionary seeing possibilities? ***CREATIVE***
    Do you focus on hard facts? ***CONSERVATIVE***

How do you make decisions?
    Are you cool and logical? *OBJECTIVE*
    Are you more people-centred? *FEELING*

What is your overall lifestyle?
    Are you an organiser (and possibly a controller)?
    STRUCTURED
    Do you like keeping your options open? *FLEXIBLE*

One important aim of this type of test is to help people understand where their own preferences lie and also to show them that their colleagues, spouse or neighbours are often different from themselves in various categories. They are then much better equipped to be patient with others and to learn how to interact with others to take advantage of each other's strengths. They gain more ability to harness the complementary aspects of personality differences rather than allowing them to become barriers.

It is not the least uncommon to find structured people married to those with a flexible lifestyle and very often visionaries are married to those who limit their focus to hard facts. This divergence can drive people 'round the bend' until they realise that the differences are part of their partner's personality structure and don't represent an uncooperative or critical attitude. Once this occurs these differences can be harnessed to bring balance and added insight. With two visionaries, and no one to count the cost, a couple could be headed for disaster. Likewise, if two conservative non-risk takers were together, they might never achieve anything worthwhile.

Jack and Carol Mayhill in their book *Opposites Attack* state that they were opposite in all four of the above categories and many of their misunderstandings were classical. But by a combination of knowing they had been joined together by a sovereign God, plus the enlightenment of a few personality instruments, they have learned to accept, work with and profit from their differences. Obviously if it works in the most intimate of all human relationships, certainly the awareness of temperamental differences can be put to use in friendships and working relationships as well.

GENDER was not addressed in the last chapter. The area of gender can cause even greater misunderstandings, and these are not limited to marriage relationships. Most of the sexist quips and banter in the work place about the opposite sex, are perversely based on these differences. Comments such as, 'Isn't that just like a man?' and, 'What can you expect from a woman?' frequently demonstrate a certain amount of human observation. Unfortunately, their negative focus doesn't make much contribution to harmony. One reaction to this has been the foolish attempt to prove that differences don't really exist.

When God said it wasn't good for the man to be alone, he didn't provide an exact replica with slight alterations to accommodate sexual relations and procreation. It seems he didn't even create Eve to have quite the same perspective; she was to have uniquely feminine insight to challenge Adam's thinking and broaden his horizons.

For well over a decade the facts have been unfolding through numerous studies, demonstrating that the hormones which produce the physical differences between men and women are also responsible for a gender bias in brain function. These findings were anything but popular when they first began appearing in the late seventies. Findings have been pouring in from researchers all over the world. In 1989 Anne Moir and David Jessel compiled many of these findings into a very interesting book they called *BrainSex*[1]. According to these authors, scientists have discovered that at about six to seven weeks gestation, a male foetus begins producing testosterone which will actually alter his brain into a specifically male 'wiring pattern' which is both functionally and physically distinct from his sister's. Not superior or inferior, but distinctly different as we shall see.

The result of this difference in wiring is both phenomenal and observable. The reason for discussing 'wiring' rather than behaviour is that the wiring produces an actual physical function which can be scientifically observed and measured. Behaviour can be as well, but we are never sure if the behaviour we are observing is caused by gender, temperament or conditioning. The function of the living brain is now observable through devices which monitor such signs of activity as blood flow, magnetic fields, and electrical impulses. One can actually watch different areas of the brain swing into action as various problems are being dealt with.

The 20 April 1992 issue of *Newsweek* explained the process this way. 'Sing, "Row, Row, Row your boat" and lift your finger when you come to a four letter word. If you are female, tiny spots on the frontal lobe of both sides of your brain light up. If you are male, only one side does.' This particular example is typical of the experiments and findings pointing out that the thought processes of men tend to be more compartmentalised, while similar processes are duplicated in various areas of the female brain.

This difference in organisation of intellectual functions is what we are referring to as 'wiring', and is the main factor in specialising the brain according to gender. The compartmentalised nature of the male brain is thought to account for linear thought proc-

165

esses, superior spatial skills and the reason little boys are so interested in the way things are made and used. The 'global' organisation of women's brains is thought to account for their more 'intuitive thinking.' Little girls are much more concerned with people and relationships and they develop superior verbal skills. Women are much more aware of 'body language,' facial expressions and what is going on behind the expression.

It is also noted that the 'cable' connecting the two hemispheres of the brain is proportionally much larger in women and has many more connections. This may well account for another common observation. The fact that emotions, thought to be controlled by the right hemisphere, are better connected to the left hemisphere containing a woman's superior verbal skills, could explain why women are more effective at communicating their feelings.

Strengths, weaknesses and variations in behaviour are of course general in nature, just like saying that men are taller than women. Statistically men are seven percent taller than women on average, but that doesn't preclude some women being taller than some men. The learning mechanisms of the brain are very flexible and many women can learn the more masculine reasoning process whilst men can learn the more intuitive approach. This fact comes in very useful when someone suffers a stroke which affects one side of the brain and leads to paralysis on the opposite side of the body. Through a lengthy period of re-learning the opposite (undamaged) side of the brain can be brought into play so bringing back a restricted amount of movement in the paralysed side.

The reason gender differences have potential for confusion in our perception of life is the fact that even though we make such comments as 'Isn't that just like a man?', we don't really believe there is that much difference. We sense that there are certain typical characteristics for each sex, but we also know that the basis of our sexist affronts are only a partial (and therefore distorted) truth. It isn't until we are exposed to the positive differences rather than the insults, that we begin to develop a factual framework on which to hang our own observations.

It is not difficult to accept that environment, genetics and gender all influence all relationships, because they influence the way we view life and therefore the way we respond to it.

SELF IMAGE

In counselling situations a poor self-image is seldom the presenting problem, and is never the entire problem, but it does seem to surface as the main problem with reasonable frequency. One can only estimate the percentage of the population with difficulties in this area, but some estimates run as high as 95% of us being affected with poor self-image to some degree. This universality needs to be kept in mind when considering approaches to the problem. We need to be aware why some people seem to 'spark each other off', and also how we as counsellors are aware of the following principles and how they are being applied in our own life.

Of all the individual issues involved in Christian counselling, the area of self-image is probably the greatest 'minefield'. There is a common thread of compassion linking the concerns of both Christian and secular counsellors - people are hurting and, for the most part, their pain is the result of a deception. Both secular and Christian counsellors are keen to dispel this deception. The fact that the secular approach is indeed compassionate masks some very fundamental differences making it more attractive than many

Christian approaches. The controversy centres on the nature of the deception and the most effective way to deal with it.

Part of the problem has been the insistence of some Christian groups that 'God views us as worms, that the human race's problem has always been pride rather than a poor self-image, and that the Bible gives us no mandate to teach on self-image'. However, the greatest problem has been the fact that the major goal of secular psychotherapy is to make us comfortable with ourselves, but the only self they are aware of is our old nature. One of God's major objectives is that we become comfortable with our new nature - something secular psychotherapy, by its very nature, could not accept.

Christian counsellors can agree with secular psychotherapy that the problem is the result of taking a lot of caustic, traumatic and probably erroneous information on board. Some of these messages were deliberately sent, others were benign messages that were simply misinterpreted, but the end result is faulty programming. However, the basic Christian awareness of a new nature in itself opens fresh avenues of approach and a complete rethinking of strategy.

We believe there are several factors essential to a healthy self-image that would not fit in with the non-Christians view of the world. These include:

> a biblical definition of a healthy self-image
> a biblical foundation of personal worth
> a biblical understanding of our new nature
> a distinguishing between performance and behaviour.

Self-image is the way we see ourselves. It implies more than just overall value, but the entire range of qualities that we believe comprise our individual worth. 'Self-image' is the most descriptive and effective term to use when considering the Christian values involved in this topic. 'Self-acceptance' can imply moving towards an uncritical self-satisfaction, and 'self-esteem' only moves in a straight line up or down, which may or may not be related to reality. Speaking as a Christian on this subject we must be more concerned with accurate and inaccurate self-images and right and wrong foundations.

IDENTITY

A healthy self-image is not a matter of ability, attractiveness or intelligence, but strictly a matter of identity. Paul's second letter to the Corinthians very clearly tells us that anyone in Christ is a new creation (Creature). Most of us take some time for this to become a reality in day to day living. We are all too aware of vast areas of our lives that seem unchanged and we may even question the authenticity of the changes that have been made.

After some 30 years as a Christian the Apostle Paul certainly knew he was a long way from perfect, and yet he knew how to cope with the tension between 'pressing toward the high calling of God' and having to deal with sin in his life. He could acknowledge failure without allowing it to derail his progress towards the goal of being God's man. His secret was that he simply didn't identify with his fallen nature, that's it - full stop! 'Now if I do what I do not want to do, it is no longer I who do it, but it is sin living in me that does it.'[2] In other words 'I have a new nature and an old nature within me - the new nature is the real me'. It does make sense, after all which nature is going to live for ever and which nature was crucified?

In a humanistic society all virtues and values are relative, and individual human worth is no exception. Therefore, most of society is consciously or unconsciously competing for significance. Many are not as concerned to be *seen* to be significant by others as to be able to see themselves as significant. Not that being seen as significant wouldn't help - it is just more than some of us can hope for. Whether we view ourselves as competing or not the fact is that achievement or acceptance (which we believe is deserved) provides a good portion of the basis for our self-image. The scales on which we compete would fill the rest of this book - anything from popularity to underwater basket weaving. The Guinness Book of Records is a monument to the fact that we can find some pretty unusual areas in which to excel. Most of the possible foundations for our self-image fall into three major categories.

ACHIEVEMENT *I am what I can do.* Achievers are vulnerable to workaholism and perfectionism and if they are successful - to pride.

ACCEPTANCE *I am what others think of me.* Those concerned with acceptance or approval are vulnerable to self-consciousness, self-centredness and 'the fear of man'. Even more precarious than 'I am what others think of me,' is 'I am *what I think* others think of me!'

ADOPTION *I am God's man or God's woman.* Fear of man will prove to be a snare, but whoever trusts in the Lord is kept safe[3]

There is an important dynamic tied in with these categories. The basis of our self-image becomes the engine of our lives - the driving force. As Christians we want that driving force to be God, but few of us are that single minded over the long haul. I (Dave) want to achieve and I want to be accepted - who wouldn't (so do I - Mike!). But - I often find it goes deeper than that, disapproval saps my confidence and even the idea that I may fail to reach a certain goal becomes personally threatening. There is nothing strange in that either, but these are symptoms of where my self-image is resting at the time.

Chances are a failure will bring on self-condemnation and I will be saying 'You did it again Dave, you dummy, you didn't really put your best into it - you don't have the inner character to succeed - you'll never change'. Two things are happening: I am allowing success or failure in a particular project to be the gauge of my personal worth, demonstrating that I am basing my self-image on achievement, and I am identifying with my old nature.

We all find there are times when we have become more self-centred than Christ-centred and we are placing more emphasis on what we own or achieve than on pleasing God. The important thing is to know the only secure foundation for our self-image and to be quick to repent and bring it back there.

BIBLICAL DEFINITION

It might help at this point to consider the Bible's idea of a healthy self-image. We have already alluded to the fact that some Christians don't believe the Bible addresses self-image, because self-image/self-esteem etc. is a totally modern fixation. The *preoccupation* with self-image is indeed a symptom of our self-centred age. It is also a symptom of our tendency to view ourselves as victims rather than accept responsibility for who we are and what we are becoming. None the less, the Bible provides a great deal of practical hand-holds on the subject.

Jesus' self-image is alluded to in such statements as: 'being in very nature God, did not consider equality with God something to be grasped, but made himself nothing, taking the very nature of a servant, being made in human likeness...he humbled himself and became obedient to death - even death on a cross![4]

Also - 'Jesus knew that the Father had put all things under his power, and that he had come from God and was returning to God; so he got up from the meal... and began to wash his disciples' feet.'[5]

In both instances Jesus was fully aware of all that he was (the highest) and yet willing to undertake the lowest possible task. One could rightly call this an attitude of humility, which is something Jesus said about himself - 'for I am gentle and *humble* in heart.'[6]

The gospel of John contains several passages demonstrating that the humility of Jesus was more than an attitude, it was also a functional strategy. Although Jesus was divine, the incarnation meant he accepted the limitations of humanity, doing nothing supernatural of his own volition. He waited for the decision of the Father to operate through his humanity by means of the Spirit. He underlined this with statements such as:

> The Son can do nothing by himself [7]
> By myself I can do nothing [8]
> For I have come down from heaven not to do my will but to do the will of him who sent me [9]
> My teaching is not my own. It comes from him who sent me.[10]

Humility has to do with the way people view and value themselves, particularly in relation to others. Humility is definitely self-evaluation terminology which Scripture casts as the opposite of pride, which is also a self-evaluation terminology. Three times in Scripture we find 'God opposes the proud but gives grace to the humble.'[11] It would seem fairly obvious that humility is the Bible's term for a healthy self-image. Naturally we must remove 'humility' from the 20th century cultural packing which associates it with inferiority. No one could imagine Jesus grovelling in inferiority and, biblically, the word was never intended to convey that.

DEFINING HUMILITY

Speaking as a Christian, any definition of humility must portray the 'By myself I can do nothing' concept which Jesus stated about himself.

Humility is actually functioning in the understanding that anything of eternal significance happening in or through my life is of God - I can't take credit for it.

Why does God oppose the proud? Because they function independently of him. Why does God give grace to the humble? Because they are reliant on him. This model of a man completely available to God the Father to operate through his humanity, by means of the Holy Spirit is the part of the incarnation message most frequently overlooked. It is however, essential to actually living out the Christian life, and central to our theme as it is the true basis of our self-image.

Being God's man or God's woman frees us from bondage to achievement or to the opinions of others, which is stressful to say the least. It allows God to harness our full potential. I am no longer what I can do or what others think of me, but a Child of the King and all that entails. However, helping a person develop a healthy self-image requires more than a lecture on being a King's Kid. It requires some very specific hand-holds which in some instances will be painstakingly established one at a time over a period of time with copious amounts of love in between. These are objective truths and the whole business of self-image is very subjective. Whenever emotions are involved the amount of time required in counselling (or actually teaching) can be multiplied by a factor of between 2 and 200. Emotions distort truth and we usually have no idea exactly where the truth is distorted or by how much.

It is necessary to help the client develop an accurate self-appraisal as Paul seems to be calling for in Romans … every man should not think more highly of himself than he ought to think ..[12] Many with a self-image problem have a tendency to determine their entire worth by their weakest quality. Therefore, it often pays to shift the focus from the whole person to individual factors - character qualities, skills and abilities. Developing some sort of inventory of assets and liabilities is always helpful. But the main emphasis must always be on the fact that real worth is a matter of identity rather than assets.

PERFORMANCE AND BEHAVIOUR

It is also necessary, at some point, to make a distinction between performance and behaviour and we don't think these definitions are taking too much liberty with the English language. Behaviour, we are vewing as the moral quality of our actions, has to do with right and wrong. Performance is the technical quality involving skills and abilities. The reason this distinction is important in Christian counselling is that performance is rightly assessed on a relative basis while behaviour definitely is not. The first across the finishing line has the most superior performance and it is obviously relative to all the others in the race. But God doesn't judge our behaviour on a relative basis. If the winner had to cheat to win, it doesn't matter that all the others in the race have also been known to cheat - he or she is still guilty before God.

It is tempting when clients state that they feel worthless to reply with 'we all feel that way from time to time,' or to encourage them by explaining that God loves them and has a plan for their life etc. It would probably be more profitable to ask them why they feel worthless. It may just be that they feel worthless because they are 'trapped' in a sin, or are nursing a sinful attitude. In such cases they need help to change and not encouragement to accept themselves as they are.

SURVIVORS

Because counsellors are compassionate people and also aware of the emotional baggage some clients have taken on board in their childhood, there is a danger that we can treat them as special - too special. The fact is no one has had a perfect childhood and well over half of the people I (Dave) have asked in lectures denied having a happy childhood (whatever that is). We have met a small number of people who did have an optimal childhood, but most of us have lived through some pretty unprofitable experiences and survived.

Some of us survived through applying scriptural principles, but most of us developed defence mechanisms and hang-ups that we may still be working through. But we survived and we are not the people we are today because we were given optimal upbringing, but rather in spite of our upbringing. This doesn't necessarily mean we bear our parents any malice, they were also the products of imperfect parenting - they did the best they knew how and still made a lot of costly mistakes. That's life.

At what point does a client become a 'special' case? Our fear is when we view them as 'special' we are also very near to viewing them as hopeless. Everyone has to bring their self-image on to the right foundation and identify with their new nature. Every counsellee with a self-image problem needs to have a biblical framework sketched out for them and the hand-holds need to be highlighted.

BIBLICAL SOFTWARE

The best way to overcome faulty programming is by developing some biblical software that can be accessed whenever the adversary begins to run the old faulty programming. Some psychologists claim we speak to ourselves at a speed of 1300 words per minute, which is very believable if one considers how much data goes through our mind in an emergency. This 'self-talk' can be a dynamic to be dreaded or a force to be harnessed, depending on whether it is allowed to re-run the same old subjective faulty programming or to reinforce objective truth. Scripture memory is the most authoritative source of objective truth. Short passages (not necessarily even an entire verse) are the most effective for clarifying the vital hand-holds. We have included some verses at the end of the chapter, but they are only examples of choosing verses that provide authority for a particular 'hand-hold'.

POINT OF NEED - POINT OF SUPPLY

One of the things accomplished in such an exercise is to make the client aware that for every point of human need the Bible has a point of supply. He or she will begin to look to the Bible for objective truth as a means of coping with negative feelings. For instance, consider how some basic longings such as belonging, worth and competence are met in the Trinity.

We all have a very deep desire to know that we belong to someone or some group that will love and cherish us unconditionally. People from dysfunctional families can feel a real void there. The good news is - that longing is fulfilled by the Father. 'How great is the love the Father has lavished on us, that we should be called the children of God! And that is what we are!'[13] We are the children of God - adopted into a family that will never throw us out or desert us. God knows all about us and wants us anyway!

We all need a sense of worth. But many of us have been severely devalued - like one man whom we counselled whose mother continually told him as a little boy that she had defecated material of greater consequence than him! This basic longing has been fulfilled in the Son. 'For you know that it was not with perishable things such as silver or gold that you were redeemed from the empty way of life handed down to you from your forefathers, but with the precious blood of Christ, a lamb without blemish or defect'.[14] The worth of an object is what someone is willing to pay. Christ didn't die for us because we had worth, but we have worth because he died for us. We have imputed worth just as we have imputed righteousness.

Our desire for competence surfaces very early on in our lives as we want to be able to tie our own shoes, button our own clothes and generally do for ourselves and even for others. Because we were all 'twisted' in various places as the result of the fall we don't all have the same capabilities. We can perform more effectively in some areas than others. But we also know that the Holy Spirit enables us to accomplish anything he calls us to do. Faithful is he that calls you, who also will do it.[15]

COUNSELLING SUMMARY

1. There are three major factors influencing our perception of life experiences and therefore our uniqueness as a person: environment, genetics and gender. *(The EGG factor)* - environment - the entire history of our life's experiences; genetics - the hereditary contribution to our temperament; and gender - the vast difference in male / female thought processes.

2. Self-image is a major thread running through most counselling problems.

3. A healthy self-image is not a matter of ability, achievement or appearance. It is strictly a matter of identity - our identity as citizens of heaven.

4. The major goal of secular psychotherapy is to make us comfortable with ourselves, but the only self they are aware of is our old nature. One of God's major objectives is that we become comfortable with our new nature - something secular psychology, by its very nature, could not accept.

5. From the Christian point of view there are several essential self-image factors that would not be acceptable to a secular world view.

a. Biblically defining a healthy self-image
b. Clarifying the foundation of our personal worth
c. Identification with our new natures
e. Distinguishing between performance and behaviour

6. The Lord Jesus' incarnational identity wasn't based on his ability, but on being completely available to the Father; thus he fleshed out humility and modelled a healthy self-image.

7. Performance is the reflection of our abilities, but behaviour contains a moral element. Both affect our self-image, but require different approaches.

8. Christian counselling encourages the client to accept responsibility for who he is and what he will become based on his faith in Christ as opposed to assuming his identity from negative input of childhood etc.

9. It is crucial that clients develop a factual basis for 'self-talk' as opposed to faulty past programming. The most authoritative facts are Scripture passages which help the client develop 'biblical software' providing crucial hand-holds on the truth.

SCRIPTURES ABOUT OUR SELF WORTH

I AM A NEW CREATION
II Cor. 5:17 Therefore if anyone is in Christ, he is a new creation; the old has gone, the new has come.

I TAKE MY IDENTITY FROM MY NEW NATURE
Romans 7:20 Now if I do what I do not want to do, it is no longer I who do it, but it is sin living in me that does it.

GOD LOVES ME
I John 3:1 How great is the love the Father has lavished on us, that we should be called the children of God! And that is what we are!

I HAVE SIGNIFICANCE IN CHRIST
Eph 2:10 We are God's workmanship, created in Christ Jesus to do good works, which God prepares in advance for us to do.

II Cor. 5:18 All this is from God, who reconciled us to himself through Christ and gave us the ministry of reconciliation.

I AM A SIGNIFICANT PART OF THE BODY OF CHRIST
I Cor 12:20-21 There are many parts but one body. The eye cannot say to the hand, "I don't need you!" And the head cannot say to the feet, "I don't need you!"

I MUST NOT COMPARE AND COMPETE WITH OTHERS WHO MAY WELL BE EQUIPPED FOR OTHER FUNCTIONS

2 Corinthians 10:12 We do not dare to classify or compare ourselves with some who commend themselves. When they measure themselves by themselves and compare themselves with themselves, they are not wise.

GOD WILL ENABLE ME TO DO THOSE THINGS HE CALLS ME TO DO

I Thess. 5:24 'Faithful is he that calls you, who also will do it.'
I Peter 5:5 'God opposes the proud but he gives grace to the humble.'

REFERENCES AND RESOURCES

Myers-Briggs Oxford Psychologists Press Ltd, Lambourne House 311-321 Banbury Road, Oxford OX2 7JH UK
Tel   01865 510203
Fax   01865 310368
OPPemail@msn.com
http://www.opp.co.uk
CWR at Waverley Abbey House in Farnham conduct the best Christian course we are aware of featuring this instrument. Contact them   01252 784700

Jack and Carol Mayhill *Opposites Attack*, Nav Press, unfortunately it was out of print at this writing.

Ann Moir and David Jessel *Brainsex,* Mandarin Press, our copy is dated 1991 - which means there is a good chance it is also out of print.

FURTHER READING

A Humble Confidence by Dave Ames
Published by Mission to Marriage 1994,
definitely not out of print.

Victory Over The Darkness by Neil T. Anderson
Published by Monarch

END OF CHAPTER NOTES

1.*BrainSex,* Anne Moir & David Jessel 1989, Although this was written as a
popular book and not an academic work it is reporting on serious and
significant work by well respected researchers and which have been reported
on in both professional journals as well as popular news magazines such as
News Week.
2. Romans 7:20
3. Proverbs 29:25
4. Philippians 2:6-8
5. John 13:3-5
6. Matthew 11:29
7. John 5:19
8. John 5:30
9. John 6:38
10. John 7:16
11. Proverbs 3:34, James 4:6 and I Peter 5:5
12. Romans 12:3
13. 1 John 3:1
14. 1 Peter 1:18, 19
15. 1 Thessalonians 5:24

RELATIONSHIPS

WHAT ARE RELATIONSHIPS?

The Bible speaks more about interpersonal relationships than any other human activity. This is not surprising when one considers that we are relational beings created in the image of God who is himself a relational being. Life consists of relating to others. The fact that relationships colour over 90% of the Bible's content is the very thing that keeps it contemporary and relevant. Likewise we find that most counselling problems involve relationship issues to a greater or lesser extent. We all struggle with relationships throughout our lives and a thorough understanding of the issues involved is important for a counsellor.

Relationships fall into many categories and go through many stages. It is helpful for our understanding to make the distinction between intrinsic and extrinsic relationships. Extrinsic relationships are usually those formed in the work place and common activities of every day living, but which don't involve us closely. We may call the people involved in these relationships 'acquaintances', 'colleagues' and 'neighbours' rather than 'friends'. Extrinsic relationships are mainly motivated around a common purpose which exists outside the relationship itself. Thus work, schooling, and even the neighbourhood we live in, may force people into relationships that they wouldn't necessarily choose for themselves.

On the other hand, intrinsic relationships exist purely for the enjoyment of the relationship - we want to be friends or possibly even more than 'friends'. The intrinsic relationship exists solely for the pleasure and fulfilment which both people can receive if the relationship is healthy. Extrinsic relationships can be enjoyed and even progress to the level where an intrinsic relationship may also be enjoyed. It is important to remember that most of the relationships we enter into are actually extrinsic - we didn't choose them. If you are a married Westerner the chances are that you did choose your spouse, but chances are you didn't choose your in-laws! In fact you didn't even choose your own relatives, but you're still stuck with them. This might help to explain why studies have shown that more murders are committed by family members than outsiders.

This brings us to another classification that cuts through both of the above categories. Relationships may be normal and abnormal, or we prefer to speak of healthy and unhealthy ones. The characteristics of a relationship are the result of the values, personalities and temperaments of the people involved. Relationships have a life of their own, which in turn affects the lives of those involved, but they are not a separate entity from the people involved. Sometimes this effect is synergistic, both parties gaining from the alliance, but sometimes it has a stifling or deteriorating effect, leading to an unhealthy relationship. Such relationships may become abusive, dependant, controlling, autocratic, self-centred, tyrannical, oppressive or unbalanced.

Another definition of an unhealthy relationship might be any relationship which does not match normal social expectations for that particular category of relationship. An example of this would be incest. In every unhealthy relationship, someone is being taking advantage of, and someone is therefore not making their fair and equal contribution to the health of the relationship.

UNHEALTHY RELATIONSHIPS

What causes a relationship to become unhealthy? Relationships begin to go wrong when one party stops working on the relationship, giving their own needs and desires a higher priority than the relationship. The selfish partner only obtains the power to impose an abnormal shape on the relationship if the other person gives their approval. Of course this approval can be given openly and freely or under duress. There can be any number of reasons why this power is given, and of course it is frequently true that the 'victim' doesn't believe they have a choice. People will comply with or suffer some pretty unreasonable, dishonest or illegal things in order to avoid rejection. Adult 'victims' of a long term abusive relationship may need to repent of certain past actions, or inactions as well as going through the process of forgiving the abuser. Conversely, rape and abuse victims often feel guilty when they shouldn't.

HEALTHY RELATIONSHIPS

We can conclude that a healthy relationship is one which is, in the main, constructive, fulfilling and beneficial to both parties.

Mutuality is fundamental - continual input from both parties is required to maintain a successful interaction. Responsibility for the relationship is mutual. The break down or restoration of a relationship is never completely unilateral. For this reason many believe that the primary cause of breakdown in relationships is poor communication. It sounds reasonable - continual input to maintain mutuality means continual communication. This would be true if our view were limited to a purely technical perspective.

Communication is the most important tool in a relationship, but it is only a tool and a tool that must be used with the utmost integrity. Therefore, it is necessary that Christian counsellors look beyond the technical factors of the relationship to the character of the people involved. It is usually the character of the individuals involved which determines the success or failure of the communication and not the other way around. More about this as we progress.

BUILDING BLOCKS OF RELATIONSHIPS

The late Tom Marshall in his book on relationships cites four building blocks for healthy relationships: Love, Respect, Trust and Understanding.[1] For a relationship to be successful all four of these aspects need to be functioning and growing. No relationship is static. I may have understood my wife yesterday, but that is no guarantee that I will understand her tomorrow. Likewise she may trust me today, but it is easy to lose that trust through actions and words.

LOVE

Love, Tom Marshall claims, is the most enduring element in a relationship. It may also be the most confusing of the four terms. This is because the English language has only one word to express what other languages, such as Greek, differentiate through several terms. The Eros love, which traditionally attracts lovers, is mainly a physical affinity - 'you flip my switches'. Phileo love, on which friendships are built, is much more a psychological affinity, being attracted to certain character qualities, but mainly common values, objectives and even down to common tastes. We like and tend to trust people who are like us - 'you're my kind of person'. Agape love, on the other hand is a self-generating love in that it demands nothing of the object of that love. 'You don't have to look the way I think you ought to look or think the way I think you ought to think - I'll love you anyway.'

Eros and phileo are terribly important in the roles they fulfil, but when Tom Marshal speaks of love being the most enduring of the four building blocks, he is speaking of agape love which is there to patch the others up when they break down. It is also the love that is commanded throughout the Bible - 'love one another' - 'love your neighbour' - 'husbands love your wives'. [2] We like to define agape as *'investing my resources in someone else's well being'.*

Agape love is the antithesis of selfishness. People often view hatred as the opposite of love, but that shows they are working from an affinity framework (as in phileo or eros) and people experiencing difficulty need to have their thinking brought into a commitment or agape framework. Agape love implies a commitment. It is almost humanly impossible to love people we don't like or who have hurt us, but as we follow God's guidelines for relationships so the power for agape love comes to us from the Father.

As we proceed in relationships we often find a progression in the type of love we experience. Usually there is an element of liking a person, an immediate attraction which may be physical - the way they look, walk and talk - or it may be mental and emotional in that we seem to have so much in common with the other person. As the relationship deepens we experience more of the phileo aspect, where a deep bond is formed in thinking, feeling and experience. This type of love may be considered mainly a soul reaction. The final stage of any relationship is the agape type of commitment, where the love is unconditional and continuing. This is clearly an attribute of the spirit and is a gift from God to point towards how he relates to us.

RESPECT

Tom Marshall sees respect as the most neglected of the building blocks of relationships - and we would agree. Respect is inseparable from love. We often speak of earning respect and there is no doubt that to some degree people do earn our respect. The Bible encourages us to be worthy of respect because it is concerned with the development of godliness. However, the Bible also commands respect with no mention of the recipient having to earn it. Why does Paul in the letter to the Ephesians tell wives to respect their husbands rather than to love them? [3] Joyce Ames claims that in fact love and respect are two sides of the same coin. Considering the basic human longings for love and significance she postulates that women are more concerned with love and men more concerned with significance. Thus when a man feels respected he feels loved. Conversely, when a woman feels loved she also feels respected.

Disrespect cannot disassociate itself from self-centredness and is seldom missing in marriage breakdown, family squabbles, labour disputes or problems with the neighbours. Gary Smalley in his book *Love Is A Decision*[4], lists what he calls *The Top Ten Dishonouring Acts in the Home.* We have included them because we have found the list useful in homework assignments.

1. Ignoring or degrading another person's opinions, advice, or beliefs (especially criticising another person's faith).

2. Burying oneself in the television or newspaper when another person is trying to communicate with us.

3. Creating jokes about another person's weak areas or shortcomings. (Sarcasm or cutting jokes act like powerful emotional word pictures and do lasting harm in a relationship.)

4. Making regular verbal attacks on loved ones - criticising harshly, being judgmental, delivering uncaring lectures.

5. Treating in-laws or other relatives as unimportant in one's planning and communication.

6. Ignoring, or simply not expressing appreciation for kind deeds done for us.

7. Distasteful habits that are practised in front of the family - even after we are asked to stop.

8. Over-committing ourselves to other projects or people so that everything outside the home seems more important than those inside the home.

9. Power struggles that leave one person feeling that he or she is a child or is being harshly dominated.

10. An unwillingness to admit that we are wrong or ask forgiveness.

TRUST

Trust is an important element in a friendship or relationship, but it is also the most fragile. Trusting anyone or anything makes us vulnerable and vulnerability by definition places us at risk of being hurt. Unfortunately, trust cannot be demonstrated without vulnerability. It could be that men place a higher value on being in control and therefore find vulnerability a greater sacrifice, hence lack of deep, vulnerable communication is a major complaint of wives, but seldom of their husbands.

The type and level of communication is the major expression of trust. A husband may trust his wife to prepare the food he eats, balance the bank account, develop values in their children and even to drive his new car, but unless he is willing to trust her with his feelings she will, to a great degree, feel locked out of his life.

Although platonic friendships seem to exist mainly at the facts and ideas level of communication, even they can be stifled and certainly limited by failure to communicate feelings. Two men may believe they know each other well enough to have a pretty good idea of the other's feelings in a given area, but the bond is greatly enhanced when those feelings are voluntarily spoken. Vulnerability is attractive because it is personally affirming to the recipient. 'He is telling me things he hasn't shared with others.'

Many husbands appear to believe communication at any level is an optional extra, totally contingent upon the needs, desires and temperament of the communicator. We like to point out that failure to communicate at the necessary level is in fact a 'breach of contract'. Every relationship carries certain obligations. Extrinsic relationships require at the least the necessary information about common goals and activities. Intrinsic relationships bear the obligation to maintain the quality of the relationship, but this is an obligation which cannot be fulfilled without communication. The Bible clearly endorses the principle - obligation presumes communication. God's thoughts while planning to destroy Sodom are a classic example of this principle. God says 'Shall I hide from Abraham what I am about to do? Abraham will surely become a great and powerful nation...For I have chosen him.' [5] In other words: 'Abraham is my partner, we have certain obligations to each other, I shouldn't keep him in the dark about this.'

People tend to change their attitudes towards communication once they recognise both the cause and effect nature of it, and also the ethics involved. Emphasising the ethics alone is reminiscent of a 'guilt trip', and there is always a certain 'trade-off' factor involved in the cause and effect nature of anything. 'Calories add to my weight, but they also add to my enjoyment.' Providing the maximum amount of enjoyment with the minimum of calories is a multi-billion pound industry. The 'low-cal' equivalent in relationships would be the most enjoyment with the least amount of work. But that would be a complete reversal of Christian values. Not because Christians believe everything should involve work, but because it is a self-centred focus as opposed to an other-oriented approach.

UNDERSTANDING

Understanding is the last of Tom Marshall's four basic building blocks and is the most difficult to achieve because it's a never-ending job. The saying, 'You can't put your hand in the same stream twice,' is as true for people as for running water. Each person changes and grows, and the person you thought you knew and understood is always growing and changing. This is especially true in a family and is the most common complaint of children. Parents think they understand the child, but are usually transferring their own feelings and thoughts from their adolescence onto their children. The generation gap can only be crossed by recognising the uniqueness and individuality of each family member.

We all have a deep longing to be understood, which is nearly as dynamic as our longings for love and significance. It may be that it is linked to our longing for love.

'If you understood me you would love me.'

'You may not approve of everything about me or agree with some of my opinions, but if you really knew me you would at least understand why I think and act the way I do.'

Most of us believe that others would agree with us if we could only get them to understand our point of view. This is why some discussions become so frustrating - others are forming opinions and planning actions which are contrary to what we know to be the 'facts' of the matter, and we just can't seem to make them understand!

Unfortunately, there seems to be no equivalent drive to understand others. Whether or not our drive to be understood is related to our longing for love is a matter of conjecture, there can be no doubt that our lack of motivation to understand others is akin to our basically self-centred nature. The song "Make Me a Channel of Your Peace", based on the prayer of St. Francis of Assisi acknowledges that this is where the battle is.

'O master, grant that I may never seek
so much to be consoled as to console;

to be understood as to understand;
and to be loved, as to love with all my soul.' [6]

The desire to be understood is so strong and may well be the most unstable dynamic in a conflict. It commandeers a false urgency which distorts all other factors, then leads to a sense of hopelessness and frustration that the conflict can never be resolved. It would therefore seem to be the key, or certainly a crucial key to conflict resolution. We have found it helpful to introduce couples to an abbreviate version of a Speaker/Listener technique developed by Dr. Howard Markman of PREP and the University of Denver. See the resource list at the end of the chapter.

SPEAKER / LISTENER TECHNIQUE

1. The speaker is the one with 'The Floor'. It is good to use a tangible article such as a drinks coaster to represent 'The Floor'. The speaker makes a statement about their perspective on a given issue and then gives the listener opportunity to demonstrate their understanding of what was said.

2. If you do not have 'The Floor' you are the listener. Your job is to listen to the speaker and paraphrase his/her statements, negotiating for meaning until the speaker is satisfied you understand them. The floor is shared, as each speaker is convinced they have been understood they simply pass 'The Floor' over and roles are switched - the speaker becomes the listener etc.

3. No problem solving. The focus should be on the problem, its effects and the resultant feelings. You may agree to discuss solution possibilities later once both parties understand their partner's perspective.

SYNERGISM AND DIFFERENCES BETWEEN PEOPLE

Synergism is something that typifies effective relationships. A synergistic effect is about two substances or people joining together to become much more effective than the total of what they could have accomplished separately. This happens with people because, being unique, we frequently have qualities which complement, stretch, challenge and augment each other.

In the last chapter we touched on personality types, referring to the Myers Briggs Type Indicator and similar instruments. This is a good avenue to consider in counselling married and engaged couples, people having difficulty in interpersonal relationships. Most of us have difficulty understanding our uniqueness, and when it is brought to our attention we still don't see our qualities as unique, but more as abnormalities. On the ugly side we often tend to see those different from ourselves as uncooperative minorities. A good understanding of what makes me 'tick' is the fastest way to understand what makes others 'tick' and appreciate that God knew what he was doing when he made us all different.

We were created in God's image, but that image is twisted because of the fall. Not only are we burdened with a sinful nature, we are physically and psychologically imperfect as well. The fact that human beings have quite a variation of abilities and shortcomings attests to the fact that we are not all twisted and spoiled in the same areas. Some are mathematically inclined, others excel in verbal skills. Some are spatially oriented making them good with their hands, and even that varies from the skills necessary for brick laying or brain surgery. Some people seem to have a natural knack for making money, while others have a marvellous ability for spending it or getting along quite happily with very little of it.

Personal relationships are built on common ground; having things in common is the foundation. However, it is not our skills and aptitudes which provide the main common ground. Really significant mutuality lies in the direction of our lives, our goals, ethics and interests. Some personality characteristics are manifested both as strengths and weaknesses in the same person. Analytical minds have a great tendency to be negative. The outgoing types are frequently undisciplined and sometimes obnoxious. The decisive can be impetuous. The self-confident leader can be insensitive and inconsiderate.

God knows our strengths and our weaknesses, where we need help as well as where we have a special ability to help others. He constantly brings into our lives others who are able to bring out the best that we have, as well as those traits of which we are most ashamed, the one for his glory and the other for correction. The primary instrument in God's development curriculum for our character is our interaction with other people.

CONFLICT

Have you ever noticed how God has a tendency of matching up the strong and overbearing with the meek and shy; the perfectionist with the reckless; the lazy with the energetic; the silly with the sober? It is not simply a case of blessed are the meek for they shall inherit the overbearing. God has a goal in mind. He is not as interested in comfortable relationships as with developing the character of Christ in our lives.

From God's perspective that is what life is all about - developing the character of Christ in us. His agenda is spelled out in Romans: 'For those God foreknew he also predestined to be conformed to the likeness of his Son, that he might be the first-born among many brothers.' [7] Once we (or our client) firmly grasp this, relationship problems are placed in perspective. When we view such obstacles as growth points, allowed or even possibly designed by God, we are much more able to respond to them with a clear head.

Jesus said: 'In this world you will have trouble. But take heart! I have overcome the world',[8] but we should not take this as a sinister warning but simply a matter-of-fact statement. It needs to be seen in the cause and effect category as hunger pangs which were given to make sure that we fuel our bodies. Such a perspective much more naturally encourages us to see what we can do to improve relationships, because we recognise God is not allowing the present problem so that we can identify flaws in our partner, but to develop the character of Christ in us. When a counsellor can get the client to recognise God is actually in control and to focus on what changes are necessary in his or her life (as opposed to the others involved) the case is well on the way to a successful conclusion.

FORGIVENESS

Forgiveness is another relationship factor which is a classic example of our need for a firm grasp on the sovereignty of God. After all God wasn't off duty or asleep when we were offended or hurt. This means there is more than a fair possibility that he had some purpose in it. Understanding the ways of God seems to cause a lot of problems to people. You will often hear: 'How could God allow it to happen', and 'If God was a god of love he would have stopped me from being hurt'.

Gordon Wilson of Enniskellen in Northern Ireland is a classic example of God using a tragedy to his glory. In a day and time when television interviews are filled with bitter statements of how suffering parties will 'never forgive', Gordon was used of God to prove that Jesus Christ does make a difference. He had the opportunity, on prime time television, to forgive the IRA bombers who had killed his daughter. We happen to know that Gordon, like so many other parents who have gained 'special qualifications' that they certainly didn't want, was still hurting years later, but the pain experienced must not bar us from the giving of forgiveness.

In addition to the sovereignty of God there are three other factors that are fairly essential to the forgiveness process.

FORGIVENESS IS 'NOT OPTIONAL'. The only other command with more emphasis in the Bible is the command to love, but forgiveness could well be considered one manifestation of our love. It is not doing someone else a favour - it is doing ourselves a favour. Failure to forgive is disobedience to God. Nothing could be more clearly stated than: 'For if you forgive men when they sin against you, your heavenly Father will also forgive you. But if you do not forgive men their sins, your Father will not forgive your sins.' (Matthew 6:14,15) A lady who was experiencing great difficulty forgiving her husband was reminded that every Sunday her congregation said 'the Lord's prayer', 'Forgive us our sins as we forgive those who sin against us'. To which she replied,- 'I know, I never say that bit' - as if that changed anything with God.

A word of encouragement to those who don't believe they actually can forgive a certain offence: Please don't feel you must give up on God or the pursuit of godliness. God is gracious and he will pardon even your unforgivingness provided you have submitted this issue to him and actually desire to be able to obey him in this area. Those who are trusting him for the grace to forgive will receive it.

BITTERNESS IS COSTLY. Spiritually, it costs us our relationship with God. We cannot get away with 'you and I are all right; it's just that woman you gave me'. We become completely and totally out of fellowship with our Heavenly Father. Psychologically it is costly in that we are actually in bondage to the person we won't forgive. We tend to think we are holding them in bondage but actually the reverse is true. Physically, failure to forgive produces stress within us which can lead to physical breakdown.

Pressure is the external force, stress comes from a wrong response to pressure. In this instance the pressure is the offence committed against us and failure to forgive is definitely a wrong response to that offence. It may sound hard, but it is true that life is not so much ruined by the sins committed against us as by the way we respond to those sins. Self-pity is destructive even when it is justified. We receive release and new hope as we forgive those who have sinned against us - however big the sin was, and however much it has hurt us.

FORGIVENESS IS A DECISION. It is a decision to release the offender from all guilt, to no longer hold the charge against them. It is a commitment never to bring up the offence again in any way that might be painful to the forgiven person. Forgiveness is not forgetting, but it is an attempt to do so and the only thing that can make forgetting possible.

Some people have difficulty forgiving because one of their defences against possible criticism is to retain a catalogue of the shortcomings of others. Others have difficulty recognising their own sin. This is the reason Jesus told the parable of the unforgiving servant in such outlandish terms, causing us to recognise how little we are asked to forgive compared to the amount of forgiveness we require.

There is another powerful dynamic alluded to in that parable. Joff Day's book, *Forgive, Release and Be Free*, looks at three words in the parable of the unmerciful servant that don't normally receive a lot of attention 'This is how my heavenly Father will treat each of you unless you forgive your brother from your heart.' Heart isn't limited to emotions, but they surely are included. Evangelicals don't go on feelings, we stick to facts. However, having feelings is a fact. The source of the feelings may not be factual, but emotions are so real they can cause physical damage.

This whole parable of the unmerciful servant is terribly important in that it speaks of accounts. Joff believes we keep emotional accounts when we are offended and we have proven this to our satisfaction as we have seen people released and marriages saved by ferreting out these back files and dealing with them.

It works something like this: we are offended in a specific act by someone else and it goes on file. As Christians we want to be obedient so we forgive that person that act - which should be good enough. But we may find the resentment returns fairly quickly and so we do it again and again. What we believe has happened is that forgiving the offence and the offender isn't as effective as we had hoped, because the really weighty file is an emotional account which has gone a step further and worked out what the actual cost of that offence was to us. It may be that we felt robbed of a certain amount of personal worth, we were robbed of an opportunity, encouragement was withheld, but we were robbed, or more importantly we felt we were robbed. Because we were robbed of something that was rightfully ours, we quite naturally feel owed. It is these emotional accounts that need to be settled.

It is considering these offences in the light of these unsettled accounts that has brought ultimate peace to many. What did that offence cost me, what was I robbed of and therefore what do I feel owed? Some of us are not very good at examining our feelings. Some of us may think its a bit Freudian and therefore not very spiritual. Psalm 51:6 says 'Surely you desire truth in the inner parts; you teach me wisdom in the inmost place.' This certainly isn't a proof text for psychoanalyses, but it is a call to examine the attitudes and motives of the heart and feeling owed is the motivation for a problematic attitude.

Once we see these accounts for what they are we can cancel them out releasing the offender from a debt that probably could never be repaid and we are free! Hear what we are saying. It is not just forgiving the offence or the offender, it is tearing up those emotional invoices for the actual cost of the offence, things we are owed - things we may well have a right to feel owed, but things that can probably never be collected. This last statement may bring up thoughts of debts that could possibly be paid, where restitution could be made or where, at the very least, an apology could be offered. There is a sense in which forgiveness is not between us and the offender, but between us and God. It is an attitude of the heart and it is God who is requiring it, and it's a good thing as well. Some we hold resentment against couldn't be addressed for several reasons. They may be so bitter themselves that we wouldn't even dare to approach them, some totally unaware they have offended us, some are so far back in our history that we have lost contact and some are dead. It is really going to God with this *emotional invoice* and telling him that we release this person and want to clear their bill completely.

Let me (Dave) share with you a very dramatic example of clearing this emotional invoice. Joyce and I were leading a marriage weekend in the West of England. During a break we got into a conversation with a couple who were, by their own admission, in a prison of their own making. They certainly had just cause to be bitter. Their 15 year old daughter had been molested by a man who was counselling her due to another traumatic incident. But that was only the beginning, he also convinced the daughter to leave the country and go to Europe with him. After 5 months they returned and the man was imprisoned for an extremely short time. As soon as he was released he convinced the now 16 year old daughter to travel to Scotland with him and they were married! This guy is 56 by the way and this is his third teen-aged bride!

Had they been robbed? You bet they had. Were they owed? Certainly! Could the debt be repaid - not really. The husband told us that he had become a Christian just before his daughter went in for the counselling and that he had never really felt the joy of his salvation. Quite naturally they had been bitter all that time and bitterness has a spiritual cost. It is difficult to fathom any parents going through such a situation and not feeling bitter.

God doesn't condone this, but he certainly understands and is ready to extend his grace to meet his timing. We had the privilege of being there in the fullness of God's timing to walk with this beleaguered couple through their prison doors. They had quite a few things on the bill they felt owed, one rather poignant item was 'I'll never walk my daughter down the aisle,' The good news is they were able to cancel out the debt in all its detail and to walk free to experience the joy of their salvation. And their new attitude was so perceptible that their daughter noticed it the next time she phoned home, and now that relationship has been restored.

Life is not ruined by the sins committed against us, but by the way we respond to them.

REFERENCES AND RESOURCES

The Speaker/Listener Technique is a combination of familiar techniques, reflecting back, negotiating for meaning and using an object to mark the speaker. The interesting thing is that the PREP foundation have done extensive research on the effectiveness of this procedure used both in and outside of a Christian context. In this the UK information on PREP can be obtained through One-Plus-One 14 Theobald's Road, London WC1x 8PF 0171 831 5261 or e-mail 106006.750@compuserve.com. You can write to PREP direct at: PO Box 102530, Denver, Colorado 80250-2530

END OF CHAPTER NOTES

1. Tom Marshall, Relationships, Sovereign World International
2. Greek has no specific authority but the fact that the New Testament was written in that language allows us to distinguish various facets or types of love with authority that we wouldn't otherwise have.
3. Ephesians chapter 5
4. Gary Smalley Love is a decision
5. Genesis 18:16 - 19
6. Sebastian Temple, Franciscan Communications.
7. Romans 8:29
8. John 16:33
9. 'Forgive, Release and be Free', Joff Day, Sovereign World

MARRIAGE COUNSELLING

INTRODUCTION

Marriage counselling has some unique factors, but many marriage problems have very little to do with marriage itself. They usually result from the violation of the same basic principles which govern any other relationship. Therefore, this chapter on marriage needs to be considered in the context of the former chapter on relationships.

The content and methods of marriage counselling carried out by Christians have much overlap with general Christian counselling. However, there are differences.

SIMILARITIES

Similarities between marriage counselling and other Christian counselling situations are:

Both deal with problems concerning human character, or the lack of a good character.

Both use the same scriptural guidelines concerning the character and plan of God.

Both use the same scriptural guidelines about how people are to get on together (90% of the Bible deals with relationships).

For everything that was written in the past was written to teach us, so that through endurance and the encouragement of the Scriptures we might have hope.[1]

The counsellor's objective is the same - to help Christians develop the character of Christ. [2]

God's demand for individual human responsibility is just as crucial.

DIFFERENCES

The major differences between marriage counselling carried out by Christians and other general Christian counselling situations are as follows.

In marriage counselling the counsellor has both parties in a relationship problem. A person having difficulties with their employer will seldom bring them to a counselling session, but most marriage counselling is done with both parties present.

There is the potential of a blow-up in the session, because some couples are volatile.

The counselling room is seen as a 'safety zone'. People will frequently say things they have been afraid to express for fear of misunderstanding or even retaliation, but they feel there is less chance of trouble with a counsellor present. This has led to some pretty horrific facts having their maiden voyage in a counsellor's lounge. (There are one or two other possible dynamics which we will discuss later.)

Problems can appear more functional or technical, often lead-ing the counsellor away from any underlying character issues. For instance, when we identify that a couple is not communi-cating, we may be tempted to teach communication techniques without attempting to isolate the underlying problem.

The marriage relationship has certain prescribed uniqueness which must be maintained, such as Permanency, Priority, In-timacy and Oneness.

Marriage counselling, *in one sense,* is not so much dealing with individuals as it is dealing with a relationship.

This relationship approach tends to limit its focus on the indi-vidual to how she or he functions within the relationship. Obvi-ously, everything about the individual has a bearing on the rela-tionship and can't be ignored. Often counsellors who normally see partners together will stop seeing them both together in order to concentrate on one partner with a deeper problem that might be exacerbated by attempting to deal with it in joint sessions. Dealing with one individual may be seen as a part of the overall strategy of a particular marriage case, but in another sense it has ceased to be marriage counselling. This individual problem could have been referred to a counsellor who was uncomfortable with marriage counselling.

Some may see this functional focus as superficial, but it can be important because it means that a couple concerned with mar-riage can begin to help other couples without feeling it is neces-sary to be able to handle any condition that may arise in the course of the counselling. It is however, better if they have the back-up of a supervisor who will help them make decisions regarding re-ferral of their clients when the counsellors are out of their depth.

THE BIBLE AND MARRIAGE

COVENANT AND CONTRACT

Marriage is both a covenant and a contract. The world pays little attention to the covenant, and the contract does almost nothing to actually define the relationship. For years, the fact that wedding vows (the covenant) were associated with specific biblical parameters provided society at large with certain traditional expectations. Unfortunately, both the Bible and Christian tradition have been pretty well abandoned, leaving most people holding a contract based on a covenant that is no longer taken seriously. These four distinctions (Permanency, Priority, Intimacy and Oneness) give marriage counselling which is conducted by Christians a tremendous edge over a similar secular situation. We have a distinct advantage in knowing what we are trying to accomplish.

HEADSHIP & SUBMISSION

It is important that anyone attempting marriage counselling has a thorough understanding of Christian family structure, particularly regarding the issues of headship and submission and knows where they stand on the subject themselves. However, correcting a couple's understanding on the subject may be a very low priority, especially if their system seems to be working for them. We prefer the mutuality suggested in Ephesians 5:21, 'Submit to one another out of reverence for Christ',[3] but we see this as a mutuality in the context of a servant-hood type of headship where a loving, serving husband is charged with the final responsibility for the overall direction of the family. However, we believe it is far more important that marriage partners honour each other.

Whether they do so because of the specific mandates in Ephesians 5 or a general mandate such as Philippians 2:3-4 (considering others more important than ourselves) is perhaps unimportant.

Counsellors can err by emphasising technique over the development of Christian character. They can also err in the opposite direction by crossing all of the doctrinal t's and dotting all of the i's. Doctrine is important as it contains the principles for effective living. But the key principle cementing marriage is servanthood on the part of both partners and not authority. We have to remember there are a lot of non-believers with successful marriages, mainly because they are, at least broadly, applying the Christian principles even though they don't know that there is a doctrine behind them.

COUNSEL AS A COUPLE OR INDIVIDUALLY?

We alluded to the fact that there are reasons for seeing marriage partners individually, but as a rule keeping them together is more beneficial and will tend to shorten the overall time in counselling. This is particularly true if you take the view that you are counselling a relationship rather than the individual. The idea that we are dealing with a relationship should never obscure a key fact. A sovereign God has allowed these difficult circumstances in order to develop certain specific areas of *each individual's life* (possibly even that of the counsellor as well). Let us look at some of the reasons for both settings.

TOGETHER

1. Marriage counsellors must work very hard to ensure their neutrality. The moment one partner senses that the counsellor is taking the side of their partner they have lost much of their credibility. There is much less room to suspect this when they witness all of the interaction between the counsellor and their partner.

2. There is less distortion of the history of the marriage when both are present. One woman told how bad tempered her husband was. When pressed for specifics she focused on his behaviour behind the wheel of their car. When it was suggested that her examples were not unusual she added another. 'He even pulls people over and lectures them about their driving.' When the husband was asked to elaborate he said, 'I have never done that.' Glancing back at the wife provoked her to blurt out, 'It's the kind of thing he would do.' We don't believe this was a deliberate lie - it was just the way she saw things. How long would it have taken to sort that lot out seeing them separately? More may be learned from observing the reactions of one partner to the other's answer than from the answer itself. Observing the spouse while a question is being answered will be a good tip-off to a possible distortion of events.

3. Marriage partners learn so much more about each other from being together in the sessions, and counsellors are able to identify attitude problems that often surface more readily during the interaction.

4. There is tremendous benefit in identifying the need for change in the presence of the one having the greatest oppor-

tunity to observe its implementation - the marriage partner. This is one of the dynamics which makes residential marriage weekends so successful - couples go back to their room to discuss the last presentation and its application in their marriage. In either setting one or both partners frequently verbalise specific changes they need to make and this tends to raise the priority of the decision.

SEPARATELY

1. When one partner is behaving insensitively it may pay to discuss it privately, particularly if the action is having an adverse effect on the other. For instance a woman with an extremely poor self-image being constantly put down by her husband wouldn't benefit from hearing the counsellor reason with him about how he was contributing to her problem. Note that there are occasions where it might pay to point out insensitive behaviour in front of the spouse, especially if it represents 'bullying'.

2. Many people have told their spouse 'I don't love you any more', but many others who feel exactly the same haven't had the courage to do so. If the counsellor expects this to be the case they shouldn't attempt to draw it out during a session with both partners present.

3. Occasionally one partner is so completely overpowering that one could never find out what is going on without separating them.

4. Volatile people often create volatile counselling situations. Angry people are frequently better dealt with on their own.

5. Occasionally it may be more effective to privately educate a wife that keeps saying 'If he loved me I wouldn't have to tell him', or a husband who believes his wife is hysterical because she can't explain why she is crying. But most of the time the other partner will benefit from knowing the counsellor has confirmed that they are really normal - its just that you may not want them to score too many points over your 'expert opinion'.

6. Suspicion that one partner is having an affair, has a history of abuse, or is currently abusing someone else, requires great discretion until it is revealed that the spouse is aware.

We have just listed more reasons for seeing partners separately than as a couple, but any or all of these reasons could represent a brief 10 - 30 minute exception to a strategy which was based primarily on seeing them together.

COUNSELLING AS A COUPLE

We won't spend a lot of time on this issue because there are a lot of varying opinions on this. Theoretically, anyone can be successful as a marriage counsellor, marital status shouldn't make any difference. After all, not every obstetrician has had a baby. Conversely, we have heard of homosexuals who didn't believe anyone who hadn't been a practising homosexual could possibly understand them. Regardless of the theoretical possibilities, we believe that, other things being equal, a married couple is the optimal marriage counselling team. Here are a few brief reasons:

1. GENDER CREDIBILITY

Not a lot of men are pleased to receive counselling from a woman, and we doubt there is a woman alive that believes men really understand them. It is difficult to counsel without credibility.

2. TWO PERSPECTIVES

The fact that men and women actually do view life from two different perspectives means that valuable insights are available to each that are not as readily available to the other.

3. TWO HEADS

It is obvious that you may gain extra insight from another person, regardless of that person's gender.

4. WOMEN ARE FREQUENTLY BETTER AT BODY LANGUAGE

Men tend to ask questions and listen for an answer. Women tend to look for an answer. Because women tend to be far more sensitive to facial expressions they are far more reliant upon them and therefore much more observing of them. Studies have demonstrated that even infant girls are far more alert to social cues than infant boys. Girls responded to more people and read facial expressions better and seemed to be able to interpret the emotional content of speech, even before they can understand words.McGuiness and Pribram, University of California, Santa Cruz, studied a vast body of literature in the late 70s and concluded that 'from infancy onwards, males and females respond in ways that provide significant clues to their later difference in behaviour'. [4]

5. PROVIDES A PARTNERSHIP MINISTRY

Many ministry opportunities in the church separate couples.

All too often couples find it necessary to go out on separate nights because of child-minding considerations. Marriage counselling can usually be done at home at a time when the children are in bed for the night. This allows a couple to function together.

MOVING FORWARD

BUILDING TRUST, GIVING HOPE, AND SETTING THE AGENDA

People gain hope when they believe the counsellor is going to address the 'real' issues. This is why the counsellors need the couple's help in setting the agenda. What, do they believe, are the real issues? It wouldn't be a waste of time to ask them to prioritise any list they may come up with. If asking for objectives and topics draws a blank because all they know is that they want their marriage straight (or all one wants is out), try asking for their expectations about marriage or their deeper longings and most fervent longings. Attempt to prioritise these.

The need to build trust is at least as great in marriage counselling as in any other form of counselling, with the added dimension of possibly having at least one reluctant partner. And it is the reluctant partner who will suspect you are siding with his or her spouse. It is usually the reluctant partner who wields the power; they are in control, because they are generally the partner with the least motivation to make things work. Because they frequently have a poor attitude, they appear to be less attractive as people, making the counsellor more naturally drawn to their partner. Be aware of this potential mistake.

POWER PLAY

Being aware of which partner has the power is important because this power frequently shifts. It is not the least unusual for the more reluctant partner to 'come through' and start co-operating only to have the other partner slack off on their effort. What has happened is they have decided they would like to be in the drivers seat for a while. We have taught this principle to counsellees simply to make sure that when the reluctant partner did come through, the other didn't start playing games.

A CHRISTIAN PERSPECTIVE ON A COUPLE'S DILEMMA

The marriage counsellor's objective will be to bring a couple through certain stages of dealing with their dilemma. They will arrive at the counselling session feeling wounded. They first need to be enlightened, then encouraged towards repentance and finally led to reconciliation, in that order.

WOUNDED One or both partners see themselves as victims. At this stage there is a lot of self-justification and believing the worst about their partner's behaviour and motives, followed by recrimination.

ENLIGHTENMENT The marriage counsellors help the clients change their critical focus from their partner to themselves. One of the most crucial tasks in marriage counselling is to bring counsellees to the realisation that relationship difficulties can only be resolved as we examine our own responsibility. *Self* is the only one we have any control over and *self* is the one God is holding us accountable for. This process some-times taxes the counsellors' ability to present themselves as unbiased and impartial, because some cases do seem a bit one sided. This is the place where prayer and creative insight are necessary to identify things that the 'innocent' party needs to work on. Otherwise the other partner gets the message that he or she is being ganged up on.

REPENTANCE Seeing one's own sin and how it hurts God, as well as our partner, demands repentance. Repentance is not only being sorry enough for offensive behaviour to stop it and ask forgiveness of God, but to formally and specifically ask forgiveness of our partner. We have too great a tendency to attempt reconciliation before repentance. To do this is to deal with the problem mainly on a technical level. Done properly, asking forgiveness is as practical as any technique. It accomplishes several things. Verbalising the offence allows for ne-gotiation in the event it wasn't properly identified. It also crys-tallises the commitment not to do it again. The offender is in fact telling the offended party that he or she has *condemned his or her behaviour* which gives *hope* that there will be a genuine change of heart. Repentance is clearing away the rubble and getting down to a solid foundation for rebuilding - reconciliation.

RECONCILIATION Having identified individual responsibility, and put hurt feelings right through the giving and receiving of forgiveness, the couple are now free to work on the problem together. From here on it is mainly a matter of helping them develop systems and safeguards to prevent re-occurrences and encouraging them when they do have setbacks.

SOME OF THE MOST COMMON PROBLEMS

Counsellors can research in advance a lot of the nuts and bolts of the most common problems, but this introductory text cannot serve as a book on interpersonal relationships as well as the basics of counselling. None the less there are a few things worth mentioning. You could use these headings as a checklist to help discover where couples are hurting.

PROBLEM ONE: POOR COMMUNICATION

Most people would expect this to head the list because we are told it is the primary cause of marriage breakdown, and it is the most important relationship tool. But it is only a tool. The primary cause of breakdown is selfishness, a matter of heart attitude and not technique. It is sometimes necessary to teach communication and conflict resolution skills, but they are to be taught as an extension of Christian character and not a substitute for it. Even if one is counselling non-believers it is better to establish the fact that successful marriage is a matter of attitude, character and commitment rather than technique.

CONFLICT AND CONFRONTATION

Because men, by and large, *tend* to be more dominant and the least sensitive to the relationship, it is often the women who is more inclined to feel taken advantage of, especially with newly weds. They lack the confidence to directly approach the issue. Ann Warren's book *They Lived Happily Ever After* illustrates this.[5] One young curate (who is now a bishop) had no regard for dirty clothes bins and his wife tried everything but straight talk. She now admits that if she could relive that first year of marriage she wouldn't assume that her husband was a mind reader. This was one of several similar cases in that book, most of which included the idea - 'If he loved me I wouldn't have to tell him'. Romantics like this need to be told that it's just not realistic'.

WHAT'S BEST FOR THE RELATIONSHIP?

The most selfless approach is to resolve conflicts, by aiming for situations that are the best for the relationship rather than for one individual. James in his letter states: 'But the wisdom that comes from heaven is first of all pure; then peace-loving, considerate, submissive, full of mercy and good fruit, impartial and sincere.' [6] Praying together (aloud) is an excellent encouragement towards impartiality. It is difficult to imagine praying for God to 'do it my way' with our spouse sitting right there. In fact praying the content of James 3:17 is a good start.

UNDERSTANDING THE OTHER'S PERSPECTIVE

Probably the most volatile factor in domestic conflict is the feeling or belief that the other person hasn't really understood our perspective. This is why we included the Speaker/ Listener Technique in the last chapter.

PROBLEM TWO: CONFUSING AFFECTION AND SEX

Gender differences and expectations about affection and sex are often at the source of conflicts. Most husbands naturally have a much more direct approach to sexual relations than their wives. Many view 'foreplay' as technique. The problem with a term like 'foreplay' is that it is seen as occupying only a very short space immediately prior to intercourse. Affection, on the other hand, should go on all day. Ed Wheat uses the term 'non-sexual touching'[7] to describe physical acts designed only to convey warmth and affection. William Harley says: 'Affection is the *environment* of the marriage while sex is an *event*'.[8] He gives a fairly shocking analogy. 'A man who growls, "I'm not the affectionate type" while reaching for his wife's body to satisfy his desires for sex, is like a salesman who tries to close a deal by saying, "I'm not the friendly type - sign here, you turkey, I've got another appointment waiting".'

PROBLEM THREE: FALLING OUT OF LOVE

The very terminology is obviously derived from viewing love as an affinity rather than a commitment. It would be unrealistic not to be concerned with the affinity, as long as we don't make the secular presumption that it is the foundation of the commitment.[9] The good news is that people can fall back in love again. The sad news is that the partner still in love will often achieve and maintain a significant amount of genuine change for many months before receiving any real response from his or her spouse. Often this is linked to the 'Power Play' dynamic mentioned earlier in this chapter. The partner who has fallen out of love is in the driver's seat and is afraid to relinquish his or her only control over their partner. The partner without the power may stop working at it if the powerful one gives in.

PROBLEM FOUR: EXPECTATIONS NOT MET

Marriage is not only a covenant and a legal contract, it is also an ethical contract as well. One person provides certain goods and services in exchange for certain considerations from the other person. 'I'll scratch your back if you scratch mine', is not a good foundational philosophy for a marriage, but we do have certain expectations. Sometimes these are realistic and sometimes they are not. Part of marriage counselling is helping couples to separate valid expectations from unrealistic ones and to identify where one or both partners may be neglecting their obligations.

PROBLEM FIVE: WRONG PRIORITIES

One of the greatest causes of legitimate conflict in marriage is failure to honour the God-given priority of our relationships. The structure on the right is meant to demonstrate how various relationship priorities rely on the foundation of those beneath them. It is obvious that our relationship with God is foundational to all other relationships we will have. What is not always obvious is exactly what it means to honour the priority of that relationship. It is simply giving attention to those things that enhance it like spending time with him, getting to know him better and total dependency on him throughout the day. It does not include the work he gives us to do. That comes later in the chart.

Public Ministry

Neighbour

Children   Family
Spouse

God

On that foundation rests the family block. This block could be divided in two because the relationship we have with our spouse is definitely foundational to that of our children. No greater human commitment is demanded than that of marriage partners to each other, no other partnership so close that 'the two become one'. However, the children are a very close second. We know we are not to 'exasperate them' and that anyone failing to provide for their needs (spiritual, emotional and physical) 'is worse than an unbeliever'. [10]

The next block is loving one's neighbour, a bit further afield. It is not just the people next door, it includes all those with whom we come in contact. It is our boss and co-workers. It is the shop keepers we do business with. It is our relationship to local government and public projects. In other words it is our testimony in the community.

The final block, Public Ministry, is: the Sunday school class we teach, Church office, counselling ministry, Christian committees we serve on. The main pitfall leaders have is confusing the work of God with their relationship with God. This automatically places such ministry ahead of all of the other priorities that actually take precedence over it. Many a clergy wife would say her husband is married to the Church. Occasionally, 'the ministry' that is usurping the family priority is more of an ego trip or an excuse to avoid responsibilities at home. That is not to say that those violating these priorities are less than sincere about their ministry. They may be truly and genuinely committed leaders, but misguided none the less. There is absolutely nothing wrong with enjoying our ministry, but the very fact that we enjoy it makes it easier to turn a blind eye to home life that may not be quite so enjoyable. We may be genuinely committed to a needy cause, but still behaving selfishly towards our families.

PROBLEM SIX: FAMILY STRUCTURE

Confusion about Christian family structure and the whole issue of 'headship and submission', has left many couples with no clear navigational plan which is why we stated earlier that the counsellor must be prepared to instruct couples in some basic principles and to challenge those with distortions which are causing marital discord. Many husbands are shoving too much responsibility on their wives.

PROBLEM SEVEN: CHILD REARING

The most powerful influence on our style of parenting is the example set for us by our own parents. Unfortunately, this is true even if we had poor parents. Modelling is such a powerful force that most of our 'knee-jerk reactions' copy even the things we may have felt were the most detestable about their parenting. Fortunately there are a lot of good books by people like James Dobson and Ross Campbell [11] to help parents earth their Christianity into the task of raising children. Parenting can bring division into any marriage for the simple reason that both partners had a different type of upbringing. But by far the greatest potential for disharmony over child rearing is in second or subsequent marriages, where one or both spouses are adopting their new partner's children. This is not just a legal problem of divorced parent access and child support. It is a problem of kids without security and parents who are pressured by it. Being divorced or widowed both have their own unique factors but the basic problem is the same. Nothing needs to be emphasised more in marriage preparation than the need to negotiate this matter in depth and at length.

PROBLEM EIGHT: FINANCES

The Bible has a lot to say about money. The main topic of financial concern among contemporary Christians seems to be indebtedness traps. Staying out of debt is certainly a crucial concern in the overall stewardship of family resources. Even more basic is the question of exactly whose resources they are in the first place. Are they ours or God's? That's not just playing spiritual games either - it colours our whole strategy.

From there we move on to joint stewardship (or joint ownership, depending on how we answered the last question). Is it his and hers or can they say without reservation that it is all 'ours'? It is not unfair to suppose that to the degree a couple fails to blend their finances - their marriage is that bit less complete. Finances represent a very tangible point of blending or failure to do so. Probably one factor enticing women out to work is the feeling that the family income was his money. The fact that all of her efforts were in the 'non-profit' sector didn't make them any less valuable to reaching the overall family objectives, but he might have been quite happy to let her feel that way as a means of maintaining control.

When she does go out to work should her pay cheque be strictly her own funds? The ideal is for all income to be thrown into one pot and thoroughly stirred until the source can no longer be identified. For a marriage to be the real partnership God intended all financial decisions need to be made jointly as often as is practical. This is the ideal but it is not idealistic. Millions of couples operate that way. Many require separate chequing accounts for certain administrative considerations, but the underlying attitude that makes the difference. The main exception to this financial oneness would be couples already in trouble due to the financial irresponsibility of one partner. If one partner is a compulsive spender, the other needs to protect as much of the family assets as they are prudently able.

SUMMARY

1 Marriage problems often have very little to do with marriage, they result from violations of the same basic principles that get us into trouble in any other relationship.

2 The marriage relationship has certain prescribed unique features - permanency, priority, intimacy and oneness.

3 Marriage is both a covenant and a contract. The world pays little attention to the covenant, and the contract fails to define the relationship.

4 Marriage counsellors find they lose their credibility once they are seen (rightly or wrongly) to be biased towards one partner.

5 Counselling couples together usually means less distortion of facts.

6 It is usually the reluctant partner who wields the power in a marriage counselling situation, and this can change back and forth.

7 Marriage counsellees usually come to counsellors feeling wounded, but must be brought on from that point to be

enlightened to the complete truth of their situation and then to repentance before they can be brought through to reconciliation.

END OF CHAPTER NOTES

1. Romans 15:4

2. Romans 8:29

3. We recognise there is more than one interpretation of this passage, but believe mutuality in the context of servant headship is in keeping with overall N.T. teaching especially Matthew 20:25-28 and I Peter 3:7

4. From an article *Just How the Sexes Differ*, Newsweek, 1 June 1981.)

5. *Happily Ever After* (Ten women talk frankly about their marriage and their man.) Edited by Ann Warren, Kingsway

6. James 3:17

7. *Love Life For Every Married Couple*, Ed Wheat, Marshall Pickering 1984 pp 136 & 185

8. *His Needs Her Needs*, William F Harley, Monarch 1994, Page 38 & 34

9. For more on Affinity vs Commitment see *A Humble Confidence* by Dave Ames, chapter seven, *The Royal Law Page 93*, MISSION TO MARRIAGE 1994

10. I Timothy 5:8

11. *How To Really Love Your Child* and *How To Really Love Your Teenager*, Ross Campbell, Scripture Press - *The Strong Willed Child*, Dobson, Kingsway

BAD HABITS, SIN OR MENTAL ILLNESS?

WHAT IS THE MATTER WITH ME?

When dealing with the problems that distress us, one of the first questions we ask is: Why? Why has this problem come? Is it because I have sinned and it is a punishment or judgement from God? Is it a behavioural problem which I need to take responsibility for and so make changes in my attitudes and actions? Is it an illness that I need to go to a doctor (psychiatrist or other therapist) about?

As Christian Counsellors, pondering these fundamental, but often overlooked, truths should increase both our insight and patience.

We are all sinners, and normally we do not receive our just rewards in this life.

The absence or presence of illness or suffering is not an indication of the person's worth, behaviour or standing before God. Some of the most saintly people have suffered terribly, and likewise some of the most evil people seem to be blessed with health and wealth.

God's judgement is not necessarily carried out in this life, but we will all be judged at the end of the world.

We all have to take responsibility for our own behaviour and reactions. We have all been sinned against, but that is no excuse whatever for continuing to be crippled by our own sinful reaction to the hurts we have received.

Illness is a complicated business, and it is usually helpful to acknowledge that our understanding is severely limited. It is helpful to see illness as affecting the whole person. When physical illness strikes it also affects the mind and the spirit. It is not always helpful to break down a person into component parts to decide where exactly the illness is.

GOOD AND BAD HABITS

We all have many habits; some are good, but others are harmful and destructive in our lives. Habits are patterns of thinking, feeling and behaviour which we commonly use in life. We can see them as a sort of reflex in which we think and react before we realise it. Habits are subconscious and only occasionally do we get a glimpse of insight into the fact that we are actually functioning under the influence of a habit.

I (Mike), can give testimony to a rather pathetic habit I developed as a young man. I used to dominate people. I constantly felt inferior to everyone I met. The cause of this inferiority complex is unimportant but the end result was misery most of the time. Most relationships were fragmentary as I was not able to react in a normal way, because I was always wondering what the other person thought of me. To overcome this problem I sought to dominate the people I met so as to no longer feel inferior to them. This slowly formed into a habit. It is not difficult to find out people's weaknesses and so seek to dominate them. I began to automatically seek ways of coming out on top in any new relationship. It was a challenge to me to show my superiority. This habit passed into my subconscious behaviour pattern so that later in life when I became a committed Christian this pattern was still there. I was no longer aware that I was doing it, so it wasn't something that I felt the need to repent of. Finally God got through to me (mainly through the frustration of my wife and her willingness to challenge me) and made me see that this sin was damaging my relationships, preventing me from growing and was a bad habit I had to stop.

HOW WE DEVELOP OUR PERSONALITIES

Who we are - what we can call our personality, is mainly formed in childhood, although it is developed and adapted through the experiences we have in later life. We can consider several key steps in the process of personality development -

1 The fusion of the genes from the father and mother at conception passes on to us a genetic make-up which consists not only of physical characteristics - colour of hair, eyes and general appearance, but also provides some important attributes to our personality. Somehow some of the characteristics of the family line are passed on through the genes, so that even when the child is adopted early in life by new adoptive parents, there are still some personality attributes from the 'natural' parents.

2 Pre-natal life in the womb is where the body is formed. It is affected by the nutrition the mother supplies through the placenta and may also be affected by any medications or drugs she may take (from Thalidomide to alcohol and nicotine). There is also increasing evidence that the soul is also being

formed at that time - and memories and feelings experienced by the child in the womb may have a definite effect on the early reactions of the child after birth. It is increasingly clear that fears and anxieties in the mother may also affect the baby in the womb.

3 Birth is usually a traumatic time, more so for some babies than for others. Whatever you believe about when the soul and spirit are formed, everything is there in the newborn child and is affected by the birth experience.

4 The stage of babyhood and infancy is a time in which the child is exposed to many influences, and needs love, care and nurture in order to grow normally. The baby needs security, regular loving attention and correct stimulation in order to develop. The growth of the personality is severely stunted if the child is deprived of these essential needs. Recent research has pointed to the long-term harmful effects on the child when the mother-child bonding is deficient. Such children are more likely to develop behavioural problems and it has been suggested that they are even more prone to developing schizophrenia.

5 The stage from being a toddler to a child of around seven is widely acknowledged as the most important in the development of the adult's personality. The parents and immediate family have most influence on the child, and many studies have shown that the place of the child in the family has a lasting effect on behaviour. The first child shows marked differences from the third or fourth, partly because of the influence of siblings, but also through the experience and attitude of parents.

6 When the person has reached the stage of a youth (8 to 15

years), the personality is more or less formed, although at this stage coping mechanisms are being learned to counteract the deficiencies in the personality. It is common at this stage to develop an inferiority complex, or to learn how to dominate others in order to compensate.

7 The young man or woman from the age of 16 onwards has a fully formed personality which changes little as the person matures.

This 'natural' personality has been formed 'in sin', that is through reactions to events and hurts which the person has experienced. This is 'normal' for all of us, we have little choice as we are all born in the image of Adam. Through Jesus the personality can become redeemed and we can mature in Christ into the 'real' personality that we were meant to be.

SATAN AND SIN

Satan's job description is to deceive and to seek to destroy the eternal lives of all people. 'Be self-controlled and alert. Your enemy the devil prowls around like a roaring lion looking for someone to devour.'[1] He knows the importance of what we said in the preceding section, and so targets the young to bend them before they have a chance to develop. This is why parents and the community have a great responsibility to protect the young. Negative and destructive elements are like the seeds of weeds which are planted in our lives when we are developing. They can be a curse spoken over us, or hurts suffered during our early lives or the results of our own natural or sinful reactions. In counselling later in life we need to root out these elements, recognising how we were sinned against, and how we reacted to that sin with these destructive elements. The process is a lifelong one in which we grow to be more like Jesus as we become more and more filled with the Holy Spirit to transform our minds and hearts into the image of Christ rather than the image of Adam.

WHOSE FAULT IS IT?

God is in control and the fact that he doesn't stop us from being harmed by sin might cause some to believe that the ultimate responsibility is God's. However, he has chosen to give us a free will in order that we might become his sons and heirs, growing and maturing and so learning for ourselves the consequences of sin. We also need to be aware of the awfulness of sin, how it multiplies and so destroys many people, including the innocent. We are called to be holy but usually fall short of the mark. The consequences remind us that we need the salvation and healing of a loving God. We need to be more aware of God's grace - we should suffer more than we do and recognise it is only his grace that we don't receive the full brunt of what we deserve.

We need to recognise that the world's way of apportioning blame is unhelpful. Perhaps this is the point of the story of the man born blind at birth in John chapter 9. It was commonly accepted that illness was a consequence of sin, but the misunderstanding was that it was only caused by personal or familial sin. Jesus points out that this is not so - the innocent suffer the consequences of other's sin, and only the glory of God can save and heal us.

The true Christian way is not to blame but to accept the reality of the situation, so leading to forgiveness to others who have harmed us and the taking of responsibility for personal actions. We must not burden people with wrong guilt. Illness may be seen as a judgement of God, but the judgement is not upon the individual person but on all mankind. The response 'there but for the grace of God go I' is a good one, as it is only God's grace which protects us from even greater harm due to the multiplying effect of mankind's sin upon us all.

A few effects of sin in our lives are:
> separation from God[2],
> loss of innocence associated with a clear conscience,[3]
> fear and anxiety,[4]
> a loss of boldness,[5]
> stress[6]
> and shipwrecked faith.[7]

But the message we have is one of *hope* - there is a way to get release. Following the apostle John's advice, 'If we confess our sins, he is faithful and just and will forgive us our sins and purify us from all unrighteousness',[8] reverses all of the above affects except the loss of innocence. However, where an 'innocent' perspective may not be completely restored, the transparency of a clear conscience can be.

WHEN IS SIN AN ILLNESS?

Illness occurs when harmful external agencies penetrate or neutralise my immune system, thus when I am strong I can fight off illness, but when my immunity is low I can catch anything that's going. It is therefore the correlation between my own strength and that of outside agencies which determines my susceptibility.

The mind and the body work together to resist illness, but when either become weak for whatever reason illness can come.

Some people are not comfortable with the term 'mental illness' because it represents the 'medical model', one in which it is assumed the patient has no responsibility for either contracting the disease or curing it. And indeed we are not comfortable with that message being assimilated, but is that true about medical conditions? Are all patients 'innocent victims' or are many suffering what may be considered self- inflicted wounds? Not too long ago it was suggested that smokers might be disqualified from publicly funded heart surgery, suggesting that such funds would be better spent on people willing to accept responsibility for their health. This idea was quickly determined to be unethical.

Some exposure to illness is due to ignorance and some to a trade-off as in the gamble between stress (with all its related illnesses) and unemployment. And are patients *never* involved in their cure? They have to take their medication, keep their foot elevated or what ever. We believe that doctors are looked on as the highly trained specialists bearing the bulk of the responsibility for physical cures and generally speaking, we bear less responsibility for our physical illnesses than mental ones. But there are still a lot of similarities.

American medics humorously talk of chronically ill patients as suffering from PPP, particularly poor protoplasm. We're not sure there is a mental equivalent, but we do know that there are many psychologically or emotionally disadvantaged people who seem to have the same up-hill battle to sound mental health. Nothing in their background seems to have prepared them to stand up to the tribulations of life. Mentally and emotionally they are weak! At the other end of the client spectrum are the seemingly well balanced people who are simply having difficulty coping with life or a particular phase of it.

SOME GENERAL COUNSELLING PRINCIPLES FOR BAD HABITS

People often come to a counsellor for help in dealing with their bad habits. In some these habits have become extremely destructive in their lives, and these will be dealt with more fully later in this section. But what of the 'normal Christian' who is plagued with guilt over masturbation, or the housewife who drinks too much coffee. Many habits start as little ones at first, and if unchecked can develop into more serious problems. Any bad habit is harmful and should be addressed and helped as early as possible. Within the Church we should perhaps develop a more open attitude to the problems normal people suffer from. The majority of Christians will suffer to a greater or lesser degree with the subjects mentioned in this section. The general principles which we need to operate may be summarised as follows.

A habit is a natural human mechanism for controlling behaviour, something like a reflex action.

Satan is always trying to stop our good habits and develop our bad ones - it is a spiritual battle for control of a person's life.

Paul's principle is one of putting off the old *and* putting on the new.[9]

PUTTING OFF INVOLVES:
  understanding that it is wrong
  willingness to repent
  assistance from others in openness
  asking for a spirit of repentance
  humility - I can't do it myself

receiving forgiveness
accountability
in failure being willing to try and try again

PUTTING ON INVOLVES:

changing the tapes, (not allowing the enemy to call the toon)
determining what positive actions are necessary to replace
the old sinful acts, e.g. in Ephesians 4:29 the person who was
critical of others now builds them up
making this new positive objective a *crucial life focus* and
remembering that we become like that upon which we focus
our hearts and minds.

This term *crucial life focus* is the very heart of the put off / put on
principle. We cannot successfully concentrate on the sin we wish
to leave behind, because that becomes the focus of our mind.
However, once we locate a suitable opposite characteristic we
are free to pour our efforts into becoming that type of person. It is
not good enough to avoid selfishness, stinginess or pride but it is
profitable to put our efforts into developing selflessness, generosity and humility.

Habits involve physical actions, but also the thinking and feelings behind the actions. You can change behaviour but still have
the addictions in thought and heart. You have to work on the
heart change and not a behavioural one, although stopping the
behaviour (or controlling it) is the essential first step. Displaced
activities will result if you don't deal with the underlying heart
problem. Most of us understand this, but it is easy to lose sight of
the more basic truth that it gives testimony to, which is: Life's
problems are the result of attempting to have our needs met
through some other source than God.

Many people are caught up in bad habits and don't recognise how much their lifestyle places them in temptation's line of fire. Counsellors can often help clients gain wisdom, to avoid temptations through the judicious use of homework assignments. For example you may ask them to 'Log the time of day and circumstances each time you lose your temper.'

BAD HABITS CAN DEVELOP INTO ADDICTIONS

Bad habits are the first steps towards addiction. Fortunately most of us stop at this stage, but the potential is there with each bad habit, perhaps under demonic influence to go on to use a substance or indulge in a behaviour which can be said to be an addiction.

ADDICTION - WHAT IS IT?

The drug addict in the gutter and the workaholic church deacon may be seen as two extremes of the scale of addiction. There is a continuum of addiction, on which most of us can be found at some time in our lives. But is there such a thing as an addictive personality? There is some debate about this, but it is probably better to recognise there are vulnerable personalities which are more pre-disposed to addictive behaviour if reinforced by learned behaviour when younger. Some estimates say that 40% of the adult population have some form of addiction, fortunately usually mild.

DEFINING ADDICTION

The characteristic stages of addictions are -

The **bad habit** stage which is typified by seeking for pleasure and comfort in actions or substances rather than facing up to issues in our lives.

This can progress on to the need to indulge more and more for the same degree of pleasure because of the development of **tolerance**.

This leads to a **loss of control** over the activity or use of the substance which leads on into the final stage of:

Addiction - where the person can't manage without the activity or substance. If there is withdrawal it leads to a variety of physical and psychological symptoms which encourage the person to start all over again. The person is **dominated** by the substance or activity. This is a form of idolatry and is always harmful.

We have seen a progression from bad habits to the development of tolerance, a loss of control and finally being dominated by something or some activity in the person's life.

The heart, mind, and soul are a battleground and even the believer will be able to identify activities, people and substances which may have occupied places in their hearts that came before the Lord, and at times may have dominated their lives.

These elements are the mental or psychological and physical components which help us identify the type of addiction. It is necessary to examine addictions individually to give them more meaningful and precise definitions. In each major addiction however, there will be a mental component characterised by activity, driven by compulsion and obsession, feelings of insecurity, depression, or gloom when the activity or substance of addiction is denied. There may also be other uncomfortable thoughts and feelings which the substance of addiction gives relief to (however temporarily).

The physical component which will characterise addictions to drugs and alcohol, is the physical discomfort caused by withdrawal from the drug. This physical control over the body by the substance of addiction is real because the uncomfortable physical symptoms can be alleviated by taking more of the drug. The addict has however become locked into a cycle of taking the drug and has become drug-dependent.

It is helpful to think of addictions in terms of the spiritual or heart component because it helps us to understand that in the loosest sense of the word we all have addictions, or are at least prone to them, and this generates compassion towards those who have been defeated by their addiction. All freedom from addiction is hard work, but if we can see what is happening in the spiritual realm we can have cause for hope and faith. Once someone has become addicted to a behaviour or substance it will be hard for them to change to a life of freedom from that addiction. However, there are many testimonies from people who have found release, but there are also many stories of people who have relapsed and not found freedom from their addiction.

A person can be addicted to a substance, such as alcohol or nicotine, or a behaviour, such as gambling, video games, or even over-indulgence in a particular sport or activity. Certain substances are more dangerous in their capacity to create an addiction in a person; heroin rates the most highly. Nevertheless, any inappropriate or excessive use of a substance or behaviour should be addressed and liberation from it sought.

WHAT CAUSES ADDICTION?

When counselling a person who has an addiction which is causing serious harm to his or her health and social well-being, a key component of the interaction will be to understand what caused the addiction. Although the full cause of the addiction may be elusive, certain factors may become clear. The value in understanding the causes is that it enables effective and focused treatment. The counsellor needs to know what can cause addictive behaviour and then to identify what has been the predominating cause in the client.

Gary Collins identifies five main groups of factors: [10]

Personality, heredity, physiology.

Past background and culture.

Present stress.

Perpetuating influences.

Spiritual influences.

The social and cultural setting will often dictate what is normal and acceptable and what is forbidden. In Christian counselling we would want the biblical view of these things to permeate our understanding and behaviour. A Christian may have a strong understanding of what is right and wrong, and this affects the will in respect to taking strong drink or narcotics. It does not preclude him or her from temptation, neither does it mean that the Christian won't turn to a drug for release under precipitating stress.

It is in the area of the will that the battleground exists as there is commonly an erosion of the will as an addiction takes hold. In the established addict there needs to be a reclamation and restoration of the will. Addicts do have a will of their own, however weak it is, and it is that which the counsellor must seek to nourish with God's love.

THINGS WE CAN BE ADDICTED TO

We can become addicted to almost anything with which we seek to comfort ourselves, or seek pleasure from. Clearly the most damaging are drugs, which range from Ecstasy to Heroin. It is beyond the scope of this book to go into all of these substances, and counsellors going into this area need much training and support.

ALCOHOL

Alcohol is probably the commonest substance of abuse to which people become addicted. There are three main stages in the alcoholic progress -

1. STAGE OF EXCESSIVE DRINKING

The person suffering from excessive drinking finds that more and more time is spent in social drinking, so there are more frequent drinking bouts, becomes preoccupied with drinking and often drinks to get relief from tension. This leads to increased guilt feelings. The person feels the need for a drink in order to perform adequately at work or socially, and social and work failures are often denied. Others are then deceived often with fabricated explanations.

2. STAGE OF ALCOHOL ADDICTION

When the person reaches this stage they notice the onset of alcohol amnesia (memory losses). Loss of control of their drinking leads to compulsive drinking, a drop in work efficiency and absenteeism. They may be drunk in the daytime and this leads to remorse and low self-esteem associated with bouts of compensatory bragging, generosity and financial extravagance. They deceive those close to them, end up in debt and so suffer increasing social isolation. They may have aggressive outbursts and paranoid misinterpretations. They justify their drinking with self-deceptions. They can lose their jobs and find the family also breaking up. There may be suicidal impulses and attempts.

3. STAGE OF CHRONIC ALCOHOLISM

In the final stage the chronic alcoholic will drink fairly continuously and suffer with loss of appetite and poor food intake. At this stage they often use cheap wines and may even resort to substances such as methylated spirits. They will suffer from confused thinking, delirium tremens, and the consequence of serious physical and mental diseases. Death often occurs through inhaling vomit, accidents or severe infection.

At each stage the person has choices. They can lead to bad consequences or good consequences. The role of the counsellor is to help the counsellee make right choices. Right choices may be hard for the person who has become alcoholic. The alcohol may have become a dominating feature of the person's life and will need to be replaced by something more satisfying and more holy. The basic commands and teachings of Jesus apply to each and every one of us. Not only will the alcoholic need to treat and cure the basic problem of the addiction, but even beyond that there most probably will be yet more painful memories and emotions which led the person to turn to drink in the first place. Christians believe in an Almighty God who can redeem our lives beyond our expectations and replace negative emotions with stronger ones based on his love.

TOBACCO

Tobacco products release three dangerous substances which cause ill-health:

carbon monoxide - which readily combines with haemoglobin in red blood cells and reduces the blood's ability to carry oxygen;

tar - which can cause changes in the lung cells and promote the development of cancer;

nicotine - a habit forming stimulant drug which narrows the blood vessels and raises blood pressure.

Obviously this physical dependency has a psychological component to it as well. Although estimates vary, heavy smokers will, on average, lose as much as fifteen years of their life. Cigarettes have a calming effect on the smoker, however, in habitual smokers tense feelings are created when the nicotine level in the blood drops. This brings on a craving for another cigarette which will raise the blood nicotine level and bring relief.

GAMBLING

Gambling is an increasing problem today. While many people consider a 'flutter' to be harmless in many people it can progress to become an addiction. The compulsive gambler may develop a life-style of begging, borrowing, lying, deceiving and may end up cheating, defrauding and stealing.

The main self-help group for gamblers or ex-gamblers is 'Gamblers Anonymous', which follows a programme of recovery along the same lines as the 'Alcoholics Anonymous' 12-step programme. In counselling situations with an ex-gambler it is worth following these steps and building on any foundation that has been laid for recovery. Obviously the Christian Counsellor would want to adapt some aspects of these twelve steps so that the *Higher Power* that we understand is the Higher Power of the Bible and not a subjective understanding.

Clearly in the Christian world view there is no room for a life of gambling. It is idolatry, in that it shifts our dependence from the provision of the Sovereign Lord to Lady Luck.

Drugs, alcohol and gambling are not the only addictions. There are numerous other life dominating problems with serious repercussions for the addicted person and the significant others in his life. Addiction to shopping has given rise to the term '*shopaholic*' which is a fairly acceptable term among professionals. Quite a number have allowed their televisions to turn them into *couch potatoes* and those who escape into their work have become known as *workaholics*. The latter are quite a bit more respected than the former, probably because the couch potatoes don't have the benefits of pay, promotion and prestige; nevertheless it also takes its toll. Exercise can even enter into the realm of addiction, the theory is that physical activity releases certain endorphins which produce a buzz. For many years I (Dave) jogged two miles a day at lunchtime and certainly felt good going back to the office - like I'd had my fix for the day. At the time I thought it was merely a psychological boost - the ability to pat myself on the back for being such a good boy and taking such excellent care of my body. And I'm sure the sense of achievement is a major factor, but it can go from building the body up to actually tearing it down, not to mention the disproportionate allocation of time and resources at the expense of other priorities. Looking at *exerciseaholics* and workaholics we see identity emerging as a major player in the game - 'I'm the guy who...'. Self-image is most probably a key factor in some of these other addictions.

COUNSELLING THE ADDICT

When counselling any addict we need to concentrate first on breaking the cycle of addiction. The 12- step approach is widely accepted as a useful framework for providing help to addicts. We recommend the adaptation to the 12-step approach used by many Christians which acknowledges the work of Jesus in bringing healing. The following approach comes from the book *Kicking It* by David Partington.

Step 1. We choose to admit that we are powerless to defeat sin in our lives and therefore our lives are unmanageable.

Step 2. We choose to believe in a holy God whose love has defeated sin and whose power can transform our lives.

Step 3. We choose to accept that Christ died for our sins before rising again, and ask him to rule in our lives.

Step 4. We choose to allow God to show us ourselves as we really are and how he created us to be.

Step 5. We choose to acknowledge where our lives fall short of God's glory.

Step 6. We choose to ask God to transform those defects in our character through the power of his Holy Spirit.

Step 7. We ask God to continue to reveal our sin for what it really is and to allow Christ's resurrection power to defeat it.

Step 8. We choose to ask God to show us clearly all those people we have harmed and to help us willingly to make amends to them.

Step 9. We choose to make amends directly to anyone who has done us wrong, whenever possible, except when to do so would injure them or others.

Step 10. We choose to make amends to others in the power of the Holy Spirit, even when the cost to ourselves is painful.

Step 11. We choose, through prayer and reading God's word daily, to know more of Christ and the power of the Holy Spirit.

Step 12. As we experience the riches of God's love and acceptance, we choose to set others free by loving and serving them at the cost of our own needs.

Some general principles for the counsellor who is helping the addicted person are as follows. A more detailed description can be found in the book by David Partington as detailed at the end of this chapter.

1. RELATIONSHIPS

As with all types of Christian counselling an open and caring relationship is essential. Often such people have had problems with relationships and are in a habit of using deceit and manipulation as part of the process of hiding and coping with their addiction. The counsellor needs to be probing in a genuine and caring way, being both supportive and challenging as appropriate.

2.   SPIRITUAL HELP

To produce a real change of heart to bring about lasting healing requires the work of the Holy Spirit in the person's life. This is usually a lengthy process - there are few quick fixes in this business. A person may do 'cold turkey' and come off the addictive substance quickly, but that is just the start of the counselling process. Confession, repentance and the in-filling of the Holy Spirit are the foundation of a helping relationship for addicted people.

3.   BE REALISTIC

Taking small steps and expecting reversals is a more realistic approach than expecting miracles and instant change. Setting realistic goals with encouragement when they succeed and support when they fail is the best approach.

4.   KEEP YOURSELF CLEAN

Contamination is always a problem for the counsellor. Be honest about yourself, and use your supervisory relationship to examine your own feelings. Have a prayer partner who will regularly pray with you, and use the 'filter of the cross' to avoid personal contamination. What this means is that before the counselling session pray that all that you hear and receive will be filtered through the cross of Jesus so as to not harm you. Likewise after the session pray for cleansing from any thoughts or ideas which may have affected you.

5.   SHARE BURDEN WITH OTHERS

You must have a supervisor and also if possible a prayer partner who is standing with you. Counselling addicts can be very stressful, with more times of failure than of success. Keeping your own faith and hope alive is an important precaution.

6.   CHALLENGE AND HOLD ACCOUNTABLE

The addicted person who is genuinely attempting to change needs loving challenge to make right choices, and to confess when he or she falls. With an open relationship the person can be held accountable to tell the truth, confess failure and be honest about their progress.

7.   HANG ON

Finally you need to hang on when the going gets tough. There will be many setbacks in which the danger is to give up on the person. A willingness to see the procedure through to the end (even if it takes years rather than weeks) is essential.

Through Christ we become removed from the world in the sense that we can believe in the eternal which lies beyond the world, but more than that we will have experienced something of that eternity through our experience of God. This Biblical and spiritual perspective is one of the keys if not the most important factor in successfully treating the addicted person. In David Partington's book *Kicking It,* he writes about the people with whom he has been involved with compulsive dependency problems. He has seen 'broken men and women, people the world wrote off a long time ago, totally transformed' (p.76). The key phrase here is that the 'world has written them off' through the natural course of events, as far as the world is concerned, they have very little, if any hope for the future. Partington continues 'Almost without exception, they all hit rock bottom. They all came to that place where they cried out to God. But it was here, at the lowest point of their lives, that God not only "saved" them but "richly" blessed them.'

EATING DISORDERS

Whenever we feel emotional pains and hurts we will seek to be comforted. Eating is one common solution to seeking such comfort. When such a mechanism runs out of control it can lead to the eating disorders such as anorexia or bulimia. The common roots of these disorders are feelings of worthlessness, low self-esteem and lack of confidence. Anorexia leads to an alarming loss of weight as the sufferer attempts to avoid eating as they have an altered body image and imagine themselves to be too fat. Bulimics, on the other hand, tend to be a normal weight, but they are secretly bingeing on food and then vomiting before it can be absorbed into the body. Compulsive eaters will be overweight and often try to diet but without success.

There are many helpful books which cover these disorders, and some are mentioned at the end of the chapter. Counsellors need to follow the general guidance -

THE CURE WILL TAKE SOME TIME

Patience will be required

The underlying emotions must be recognised

Referral to medical help is often needed, especially if there is excessive loss of body weight.

Work will need to be done to help the sufferer recognise that they have a problem

Naming the problem and acknowledging the causes is important

Help the person to understand that they have the ability to make right choices

Set realistic goals, and be prepared for failures

Help the sufferer to recognise how they have been sinned against

This will lead into times of forgiveness for those who have hurt them. (Help them cancel out the 'emotional invoice as discussed in chapter 10')

Counteract negative thoughts and replace them with correct biblical ones

Help them to the right foundation for their self-worth

Speak out the truth

With all of the addictive disorders the counsellor will need to be prepared to seek expert and professional help. Do not be afraid to ask for help; it is not a sign of your own failure. Open communication between the different people attempting to care for the person will also be needed. Above all else intercede and seek for the Holy Spirit to lead and guide the whole process.

NOTES, RESOURCES AND FURTHER READING

We recommend the following books for those who wish to read more about counselling the various addictions.

WILKINSON, Helena *Beyond chaotic eating: a way out of anorexia, bulimia and compulsive eating*. Marshall Pickering, 1993. An up-to-date and readable book on eating disorders. The underlying contributory factors, including family background, sexuality struggles and emotional hunger, are explored. Guidelines for full recovery from chaotic eating are given.

BUCKROYD, Julia *Eating your heart out* Optima 1989

HART, A.D. *Healing life's hidden addictions*. Crossway books, 1990. Especially chapter 11 - Addictions to food.

PARTINGTON, David. *Kicking it*. Frameworks, 1991.

Makes easy reading for those struggling with an addiction in their life, and those who have to care for those with addictions. This book is free from technical jargon and gives a Christian approach to beating life-dominating dependency problems. By focusing on the power of God's Spirit to break the grip of the addiction and understanding the redemptive work of Jesus Christ, the individual is encouraged to find new meaning and purpose in life.

OVERCOMERS, is an Outpatient Recovery Programme used by Yeldall Manor. It is a Programme based on the twelve step process for overcoming addictions and life-controlling problems. Currently it is being used to great effect in many local churches simply as a discipleship tool to help believers along in their journey towards attaining wholeness, spiritual maturity and godliness. Contact: Bridges International, 21a Bridge St. Town Mills House, Andover, Hampshire SP10 1BL Phone 01264 338999

ARTERBURN, Stephen *Addicted to love*. Eagle, 1991.

KELLER, John E. *Ministering to alcoholics*. Revised edition. Augsburg, 1991.

RUSTON, George *Alcohol and other drugs*. Scripture Union, 1991

PULLINGER J. *Crack in the Wall: The Life and Death of Kowloon Walled City*. Hodder & Stoughton, 1989.

Jackie Pullinger writes - 'The Walled City is a consistent reminder of God's unfailing love for those who really have "hit the bottom", those who are rejected by their own families and society, those who have no hope, no future, nothing in life. To see these hardened addicts turn to receive the love of Jesus has for them, to see their faces begin to shine with hope is a wonderful experience, to have the privilege of participating in that process by praying for them is very humbling. In them I have found some of the most gentle, loving, caring and finest individuals I have ever come across. I see how much they have changed, not by their own willpower, but by the grace of God. They know that they are set free from their addiction, but they are set free from their past as well.'

CLINEBELL, H. *Understanding and Counselling the Alcoholic*: revised edition. Abingdon Press, 1968.

COLLINS, G.R. *Christian Counselling: A Comprehensive Guide*. Revised and expanded. Word, 1989.

KESSEL, N. and WALTON, H. *Alcoholism.* MacGibbon & Kee, 1966.

END OF CHAPER NOTES

1. 1 Peter 5:8   2. Isaiah 59:2   3. Genesis 3:7 & 11

4. Genesis 3:8-10   5. Proverbs 28:1   6. Psalm 32:1-4

7. 1 Timothy 1:18-19   8. 1 John 1:9

9. Ephesians 4:17-32, Galatians 5:13-26 and Romans 12:21

10. *Christian Counselling: A Comprehensive Guide,* Collins, G ,Word 1989, chapter 33

PRACTICAL ISSUES IN COUNSELLING

In this chapter we look at some of the practical issues surrounding the counselling setting. At first these may sound rather boring and unnecessary, but they are essential if you are to become at all professional in your ministry. The main issues to be dealt with are:

> **Ethics of counselling**
> **Legal aspects of counselling**
> **Managing the process of counselling**
> **Supervision for the counsellor**
> **Accreditation**

Before embarking on what can only be a brief summary of these practical aspects of counselling, we wish to point out that the latest positions with regard to ethical, legal and accreditation issues should be obtained directly from the Association of Christian Counsellors (ACC). This organisation exists to support and inform Christian counsellors as well as protect counsellees from poorly trained and unethical counsellors. The British Association for Counselling (BAC) is the main secular organisation providing the same service. Whatever is written in this chapter should only be taken as a guide - up-to-date information is available through either the ACC or the BAC.

ETHICS OF COUNSELLING

The ethical basis of Christian Counselling is similar to all other forms of counselling. The following brief notes act as an introduction to the topic.

EXPLOITATION

Care must be taken not to exploit people who come for help because many of them are in a vulnerable state and may be less able to resist pressures put upon them. We must be aware that in early meetings people may appear to agree with what we say because they do not feel able to disagree or challenge us. We can assume that the agreement of the client has been obtained, but we should always check to ensure that they are still understanding and in agreement with the actions we are taking. Christians need to be especially careful of appearing to evangelise or preach at people within the counselling contract. The person may well need both of these activities, but they are best given outside the counselling situation, and preferably by someone other than the counsellor. In addition it is obvious to point out that counsellors must not exploit their counsellees financially, sexually, emotionally, or in any other way. Even Christians can fall into the trap of too intimate contact with their clients, and both Satan and the world are only too happy to trip up Christian counsellors who step outside the strict ethical guidelines which are there to protect both counsellor and client.

CLIENT INTEGRITY

The integrity of the counsellee must be maintained at all times. Counsellors are responsible for working in ways which promote and increase the control a person has over his or her own life. This implies that we make every effort to respect the counsellee's ability to make their own decisions in the light of their own beliefs and values. A counsellor should not normally act on behalf of one of their counsellees, but if they do, it should be only at the express request of the counsellee, and preferably confirmed in writing.

CLIENT SAFETY

The safety of the counsellee must be safeguarded and all reasonable steps taken to seek appropriate medical or legal assistance. Counsellors should take all reasonable steps to ensure that the counsellee suffers neither physical nor psychological harm during counselling. Above all this implies that the client will be referred on to other professional or medical experts when the counsellor has doubts about his/her own abilities to safely deal with the problems presented by the client.

MAINTAIN CORRECT RELATIONSHIP

The basis of the relationship between the counsellor and counsellee should be explicit, preferably written, prior to commencement of counselling. During this initial stage of setting a contract between the counsellor and the client, the boundaries of the counselling relationship should be set. This is especially important if there is already some other kind of relationship in existence. This is likely if the two attend the same church or routinely meet in social situations. There is nothing worse than being approached by clients outside the sessions, when it is inappropriate and even potentially harmful to attempt to mix counselling help with social intercourse. Over-dependence should also be avoided, and contact with a client may need to be terminated for a while so that other support mechanisms may be strengthened.

INFORMED CONSENT

If other counsellors or trainees are present during a counselling session then the consent of the client must be obtained. Informed consent implies that the client understands all of the implications of what they are consenting to, and they are given the space and ability to refuse without affecting the counselling relationship. Clearly if the counsellor believes that a certain action is necessary, and the client disagrees, then this should be recorded in writing.

RECORDS

Records of counselling sessions should normally be kept and the counsellee should be made aware of this. As already mentioned in chapter seven, anything written down about the client is now legally to be made available for their inspection if they so request. This means that we should never write down something that is not completely true, over stated or is a personal opinion not backed up by observation or explanation. At the counsellee's request information should be given about access to these records, their availability to other people, and the degree of security with which they are kept. In particular, if tape or video recording is included, this must be expressly with the counsellee's written consent.

CONFIDENTIALITY

Confidentiality must be observed at all times. Any written records must be kept safely in a way which prevents access by other people. No identifiable details should be discernible when the counsellor is talking about their work, whether to a supervisor or in a public meeting. Christian counsellors need to be particularly aware that the right to confidentiality must not be waived in the context of asking for prayer support within the church setting. Just using a false name may not be sufficient if the other details enable the listeners to identify who the person is likely to be.

LEGAL ASPECTS OF COUNSELLING

The law is always a minefield which the counsellor hopes to never have to enter. However, Christian counsellors have been dragged into legal confrontation, and if it does happen then expert advice should be taken straight away. The following brief guidelines are meant to help you avoid problems, but full guidance should be sought from one of the counselling organisations.

Counsellors should work within the law at all times. This is an obvious truism, but many people are vague as to what the law demands of the counsellor. As mentioned above, counsellors should take all reasonable steps to be aware of current laws affecting the work of the counsellor. A counsellor's ignorance of the law is no defence against legal liability or penalty.

Generally speaking, there is no legal duty to give information spontaneously or on request until instructed to do so by a court. Refusal to answer police questions is not an offence, although lying could be. In general terms, the only circumstances in which the police can require an answer about a counsellee, and when refusal to answer would be an offence, relates to the prevention of terrorism and possibly also in cases where serious abuse has occurred to children. It is good practice to ask police personnel to clarify their legal right to an answer before refusing to give one. The police do have powers to seize confidential files if they have obtained a warrant from a circuit judge. Hindering the police from taking them in these circumstances may be an offence.

There is no legal obligation to answer a solicitor's enquiry or to make a statement for the purpose of legal proceedings, unless ordered to do so by a court. There is no legal obligation to attend court at the request of parties involved in a case, or at the request of their lawyers, until a witness summons or subpoena is issued to require attendance to answer questions or produce documents. Counsellors should seek legal advice and members may contact the ACC or BAC if they are in any doubt about their legal rights and obligations before acting in ways which conflict with the agreement made with counsellees who are directly affected.

Once in a witness box, there is a duty to answer questions when instructed to do so by the court. Refusal to answer could be punished as contempt of court unless there are legal grounds for not doing so. It has been held that communications between the counsellor and counsellee during an attempt at 'reconciliation' in matrimonial cases are privileged and thus do not require disclosure unless the counsellee waives the privilege. This does not seem to apply to other kinds of cases.

THE COUNSELLING CONTRACT

It is important for clear contracts to be made whenever feasible. If the client has sought out a Christian counsellor, it will be argued that the counsellor is in a different position from a person who is merely a friend. The Law makes a distinction between a person who sits in an office and makes an appointment of a semi-official nature to see a client, and a person who chats in a cafe to an acquaintance. The person who gives a friend advice about how to conduct their relationships is in a different position to somebody who agrees to help with counselling advice.

It is vital for the counsellor to set out the boundaries of the counselling relationship and this is best done by preparing a simple agreement with a client which clearly says why the counsellor is involved and what he or she will (and will not) do. It is best to prepare a very short agreement which clients should be asked to sign after the agreement has been read to them or they have had a chance to read it themselves. *See Appendix C for a sample contract.*

If you are involved in setting up a counselling service, it is important to consider situations which could be very compromising for a counsellor. By and large an agency should be careful about using as counsellors anyone who has a criminal record which is not covered by the Rehabilitation of Offenders Act. That Act classes certain types of offences into categories whereby the offence can be ignored, for most purposes, once a period of time (up to ten years) has elapsed. If in doubt consult the ACC or BAC. A person with a criminal record acting as a counsellor is at a disadvantage, if any part of the counselling relationship is ever raised in court in criminal or civil proceedings. This can arise quite innocently from the counsellor's point of view. The problem of a counsellor with a criminal record needs to be looked at quite carefully and the agency should ensure, if they are to use a person with a criminal record involving dishonesty, certain types of assault and sexual offences, that clients are aware of the position.

CAN A CLIENT SUE A COUNSELLOR IF THEY GIVE ADVICE FREE OF CHARGE?

Basically - yes. If the client, or more usually their relatives, feel that harm has been done, either intentionally or unintentionally, then they may have grounds for complaint. On the whole the counsellor giving care without a fee is in the same position as one who charges. Even if there is no contract between the counsellor and the client, or no actionable breach of the contract, then the general law relating to negligence may apply. This was summarised well, in a case where the Judge said: 'You must take reasonable care to avoid acts or omissions which you can reasonably foresee would be likely to injure your neighbour.'

The avoidance of negligence claims involves a lot of common sense. Payment, or the lack of it, is irrelevant to a claim based on negligence. It is necessary to ask what a reasonable counsellor would have done, and common sense will sometimes come to your help in deciding what is reasonable. For example a counsellor who notices very strange behaviour during an interview with a client, and who fails to ask the client if he can help by calling a doctor, may well find himself in difficulties.

Since the court will ask what a reasonable counsellor would have done in the circumstances, the counsellor will be protected if the wide body of professional opinion accepts that the methods used by the counsellor were valid and generally appropriate. One of the functions of counselling associations such as the ACC or BAC is to set up guidelines for counsellors. A counsellor who follows those guidelines will be in a much better position than one who has not bothered to digest and then follow them.

ABUSE OF CHILDREN

There has been a significant increase in harm to children over recent years with the disintegration of the traditional family and the isolation of one-parent families. Emotional harm to children is often caused by the confusion flowing from broken relationships. Most of us believe that the local authority (and for that matter the police) will always act compassionately and responsibly and in the best interest of the child in the context of the family. Unfortunately, some local authorities and a few police officers have demonstrated otherwise. The Children's Act 1989 has tried to rectify this position by giving the Court more powers and it is to be hoped that the Court will provide a framework for supervening common sense.

A counsellor may find himself in a position where he has suspicions that all is not well in the family that is receiving counselling. He may be faced with a choice if he knows that a family needs appropriate help. By way of example, a counsellor may be told of a curious medical problem in a child. It may be described as soreness in the region of the genitalia. Such a counsellor is not under a duty immediately to report a case of suspected child abuse, but common sense would indicate that a strong and recorded advice to seek medical help should be given to the client. If it becomes clear that the client has major problems and there are indicators that the client may have been involved in child abuse, then it is important to warn the client at an early stage that the counsellor has no immunity or privilege. The counsellor must explain that if questioned by the police he is under a duty to disclose what he has heard.

MANAGING THE COUNSELLING PROCESS

To summarise what is said throughout this book - any counsellor should consider the following checklist in each counselling encounter.

Is the client clear that a counselling contract is being made?

Is that contract in writing, and understood, agreed and signed by the client?

Has the counsellor explained about any records which will be kept and matters of confidentiality?

Does the client understand what the boundaries of this counselling contract are?

As the counselling proceeds, am I happy that I have the expertise to deal with the problems, or is referral to another person indicated?

Is the client giving any signs that they are unhappy with the counselling being given?

Are the objectives we have set being reached, and is satisfactory progress being made?

Am I continuing to be effective in this counselling process, or do I need to refer the client to someone else? *(Yes we realise that, in effect, we have said the same thing twice, but it is so important to always practise within your own competence and ability - never be afraid to admit that you need help).*

When should we end this counselling process?

Am I receiving adequate supervision while giving counselling help?

SUPERVISION AND THE COUNSELLOR

All counsellors should be adequately supervised. This is best carried out on a regular basis in a one-to-one situation with an experienced counselling supervisor. It is wise advice to receive at least one hour of supervision for every 10 to 20 hours of counselling given. Occasionally as an alternative, or more usually as a supplement, the counsellor can join a small group of other counsellors in supervisory meetings. Guidelines on supervision are given by the ACC and the BAC and courses to train supervisors are essential if you find yourself giving supervision to other counsellors.

In addition to supervision the counsellor should also consider their needs for both on-going training, and personal counselling or pastoral support.

In a supervisory relationship the counsellor will share both the practical aspects of their counselling, and also their own feelings and anxieties about the counselling they provide. It is not necessary to divulge confidential information, but the counsellor should be prepared to explain the sort of problems they are dealing with and how effective they are.

If the supervisor is not a Christian it is also recommended that the Christian counsellor should have pastoral cover as many times there will be spiritual attack or pressure mounted on the faith and beliefs of the counsellor which should be faced openly.

COUNSELLING ASSOCIATIONS

All counsellors should be suitably accredited and belong to one of the counselling organisations. The ACC has given a lot of thought to the process of accreditation which covers all types of Christian counselling from the basic level of caring right up to supervision and teaching. The latest requirements should be obtained from the ACC who will be pleased to give advice and support to all Christian counsellors.

The counselling associations are concerned with four main areas. All counsellors should belong to one of the national counselling associations. In the UK at the present time the BAC and ACC are the two main ones and we describe the main objectives of the ACC to indicate why such organisations are an invaluable resource for the counsellor.

ACCREDITATION

At present any one in the UK can counsel without any type of accreditation, but we all know that there are a lot of incompetent counsellors practising and the Christian Church is no exception. In fact the religious nature of the Church causes some to feel that training and accreditation are not very spiritual - 'after all the apostles weren't accredited'. However, there is a strong move in the secular community to bring vocational standards into counselling. Television documentaries are beginning to appear demonstrating that anyone can go into the counselling business. It doesn't take a visionary to predict a tightening down and a raising of standards. Shouldn't Christians take their ministry of counselling seriously?

RECOGNITION OR VALIDATION OF TRAINING COURSES

Counselling courses are offered by a large variety of Christian ministries throughout the UK. Normally the ACC itself does not offer training courses although it has organised some where current training has been deficient. This is perhaps the most noticeable transformation of the Christian counselling landscape in Great Britain. At one time various organisations developed courses of any length that took their fancy. A basic course might be 5,10 or 100 hours and an advanced course for one group might be a repeat of someone else's basic course. The ACC has some clear guidelines as to the type and scope of material which ought to be included at various levels and this is under constant revision. Maintaining the validity of a counselling course isn't an easy task for the teaching organisations, but it is a real service to the student and their clients.

DEALING WITH COMPLAINTS AGAINST COUNSELLORS

It is sad to record that complaints are made against Christian counsellors and the ACC has set up a complaints procedure to sort out these complaints. If a complaint is upheld against an accredited member, the Association may withdraw membership from that counsellor. This is part and parcel of a professional body policing itself and is the very thing that maintains credibility.

PROMOTING ALL ASPECTS OF THE CHRISTIAN COUNSELLING MINISTRY

The Association has representative members from around 100 member organisations who make up its governing council. From this council members are appointed to the board of directors. This board is charged with overseeing the accreditation and training committees as well as deliberating on legal and ethical issues around the ministry of counselling.

EPILOGUE

Epilogues frequently do not add anything of real substance to a book and in fact they often detract from it, therefore they are usually not a good idea. However, we thought it would be good to have one more shot at the main purpose of this book - to express from another perspective the difference between Christian and non-Christian counselling.

It is impossible to make that distinction without offending someone. Indeed it would be prudent to avoid the issue all together. After all there are very few counsellors that don't actually help their clients and Christian counsellors would be the first to admit that of those who might actually exacerbate their client's problems it is the Bible thumpers that scare us the most. Naturally, at least a part of the reason they attract so much of our concern is that Bible thumpers have the greatest potential to damage the reputation of all Christian counselling and even Christianity in general.

Several years ago a very anti-Christian counselling article was published in a Christian magazine offering the logic: 'When I go to the butcher, I'm not concerned with whether or not he is a Christian, but in the quality of the meat he is selling me.' Indeed if the issues in counselling were similar to: 'What's the difference between Christian and non-Christian welding', there would be little point in writing a book on the subject.

On the other hand, we don't think any yard stick that could possibly be developed to measure the Christian pedigree of a given counselling model could be applied across the board in every counselling transaction. This is because sometimes the issues at stake are rather 'nuts and bolts' practical considerations of perception or wrong focus where common sense and common grace are the order of the day.

Undoubtedly the factor or factors at the core of questions like: 'What constitutes Christian counselling?', or 'How Christian is your counselling?', lie in the material discussed under the headings of theology, anthropology and methodology. The stronger our belief that humanity is created in the image of God, to function in concert with God, the greater our tendency will be to see human problems as arising from actions and attitudes which are at cross purposes with that design.

In a recent article on Christian counselling one counsellor was quoted as saying: 'My practice is to work within the client's own value system.' This probably wouldn't create a lot of heartburn among Christians reading the article, especially being aware of the amount of 'marketplace counselling' being done by Christian counselling agencies. Secular people coming to Christians expect to have their values respected. This same counsellor went on to say: 'Even with Christian clients I would never use the Bible in a directive way'.[1] Reading the article one could have the utmost respect for this woman pouring her heart and life into the task of relieving human suffering. As we have mentioned early on in this book we are extremely grateful for the thousands of counsellors willing to make this investment as an act of Christian love. If a person uses their totally secular skills to help their fellow humans is that not an act of love? Are we not called to love one another? The answer to both questions is obviously yes as is the answer to the next question. Will I be a more effective lover if I am a better butcher, welder or counsellor? And finally, will I be a more effective counsellor at least with Christian clients if my counselling is truly Christian? We think the answer to that one is yes as well.

This circles right back to the question of what makes counselling truly Christian. We think the Bible makes a pretty good case that basic human nature is independent, rebellious and self-pleasing. Even those of us who are glad to identify ourselves as members of God's family often demonstrate that we don't really want to walk too close to him, because he might interfere with our plans. Jeremiah puts it this way,

> 'My people have committed two sins: They have forsaken me, the spring of living water, and have dug their own cisterns, broken cisterns that cannot hold water.'[2]

This is so graphic. God is the Spring of Living Water and a spring is a dynamic rather than a static thing. Living water soon stagnates when stored, but we can't seem to take that concept on board. We want to fill our flasks and thermoses so as to allow us a good measure of independence from God without relinquishing our living water. 'Lord I'll have a pint of living water and please help me to keep the fizzy, sparkly stuff locked in'.

If we believe that basic human nature is independent, rebellious and self-pleasing and that it is this which gives all of us our basic predisposition to be cistern diggers, it would be hard to exclude this from our checklist of possible causative agents when analyzing problems. If we suspect that the root of the client's current problem is that he or she has algae growing in their living water, wouldn't it be a great act of love to open our Bibles and explain this to our client? If human problems do occur as we become separated from God, wouldn't it be wonderful to have someone equipped to help us isolate the point at which this all began to go wrong? We would consider a person so equipped to be a Christian counsellor. At the same time we would have to consider any counselling that didn't help the client to deal with their problems at their most fundamental level, that of getting plumbed back into the stream of living water, to be something less than Christian.

We are not saying that people who do not deal with their clients on this level are less than Christian. There has, unfortunately, been the implication that those who do specialize in helping their clients deal with the spiritual roots of their problems are doing something other than counselling. One of the reasons for writing this book is to say that it's all right to be a counsellor who isn't afraid to point people to solutions that are in their Bibles. As we have also noted the word counsel and variations of it is used between 53 and 125 times in the Bible depending on which translation one is using. We really don't think Christians need to look for a new word to describe their ministry but Jeremiah might be pleased if we called ourselves plumbers!

Please don't neglect to read Appendix A.

END NOTES

[1].We are not identifying this quote out of respect for both the magazine and the counsellor being quoted. The purpose of the quote was an example and not a witch hunt into others with differing opinions.
[2].Jeremiah 2:13

APPENDIX A

MAIN SCHOOLS OF SECULAR COUNSELLING

First we must stress that this review of secular counselling is subjective and extremely limited. Any author has particular preferences and prejudices so we strongly recommend that the serious student of counselling refers to the original books as detailed at the end of the chapter. The majority of counselling approaches used in the western world are based on one of three approaches - humanistic, psychological and behavioural.

HUMANISTIC THEORIES OF COUNSELLING

The humanistic theories of counselling are so named because they are based on the Humanistic set of beliefs. It is worthwhile reviewing what these are if you are not familiar with them. The following are quotes from the Humanist Manifesto affirming the five basic tenets of humanism.

1. 'Humanists regard the universe as self-existing and not created ... we find insufficient evidence for belief in the existence of a supernatural ... as non-theists, we begin with humans and not God. No deity will save us, we must save ourselves'

2. 'Humanism believes that man is a part of nature and that he has emerged through an evolutionary process. There is no credible evidence that life survives the death of the body.

3. 'We affirm that moral values derive their source from human experience. Ethics are autonomous and situational, needing no theological or ideological sanction.'

4. 'Human life has meaning because we create and develop our own futures. We strive for the good life here and now. Individuals should be encouraged to realise their own creative talents and desires. We believe in maximum individual autonomy consistent with social responsibility.'

5. 'We have reached a turning point in human history where the best option is to transcend the limits of national sovereignty and to move towards the building of a world community. We look to the development of a system of world law and a world order based upon trans-national federal government.'

The four most popular methods of counselling using the humanist approach are the Rogerian, or person-centred approach; Reality Therapy; Rational-Emotive therapy, and Transactional Analysis.

ROGERIAN PERSON-CENTRED COUNSELLING

The three basic assumptions on which Carl Rogers based his humanistic approach to counselling are:

1. A subjective frame of reference: A person's behaviour can be observed either from an external frame of reference, which may be called objective, or from the internal frame of reference, the subjective view. The Rogerian view is that only the person's own perceptions and experiences are of importance. This has led to the term *person-centred* counselling being applied to this approach.

2. The actualising tendency: The actualising tendency according to Rogers is the single motivating drive within each person which represents the tendency to maintain, enhance and reproduce themselves above all else. This actualising tendency is viewed as a positive force which assumes that man has the capacity to guide, regulate and control himself without external input.

3. Experience, Perception and Awareness: Great stress is laid on the ability to correctly perceive and become aware of experiences. Most of the time we are not aware of the way in which we experience the world around us. Perceiving is therefore becoming aware of the stimuli and experiences in our lives, which may or may not correspond with 'reality' because of defensive denials and distortions which have arisen due to past events in our lives.

Carl Rogers has had a major impact on counselling over the last 50 years. Many of the concepts and practices used would, at first sight, not be out of place in a Christian approach. Indeed many Christians, who believe that real answers can only be found in the *objective*, are indebted to his concept of the *subjective* as it has helped them approach clients in a sensitive way which has brought new hope. However, because he is so influential, successful and apparently true, we need to very carefully examine some of the activities and consequences of client-centred therapy.

In Roger's view *'person centred' does not mean* that the person is at the centre of the counselling process, but rather that the subjective view of the person is paramount - that is there is no external or objective standard to judge against. This is what the Bible would call 'doing what is good in their own eyes', and is therefore completely opposed to the biblical view that what a man thinks for himself is less important than what God thinks. Of course it is of importance how a person sees each situation and some Christian counsellors are, unfortunately, oblivious to this. However, the Christian world-view maintains that God has provided external, objective reference points to guide us on our life journey and help us in responsible decision making. If we deny that God exists then there is no absolute truth or authority, so God has to be replaced by something else, which tends to be either the individual's own ideas or those of the state. The actualising tendency, although true up to a point, therefore seems to state that man is his own saviour.

When looking at the goal Rogers has for people there is a very New Age feel about it, with such statements being used as -

Openness to the world, both inner and outer.
Scepticism regarding science and technology.
Attitude of closeness towards nature.
Trust of the authority within.
A yearning for the spiritual, (but without the true and living God).

In our view the humanistic beliefs under-girding Rogers' 'Person-centred' approach to counselling are fairly evident. He seems to centre around the notion that 'man is basically good and the answers are contained within him' and 'there is no absolute truth'. While many of the concepts and methods used sound correct, we believe they are essentially flawed and should only be used with caution.

REALITY THERAPY

Reality therapy was largely developed by William Glasser, a psychiatrist from California. It emphasises the importance of acknowledging reality as the basis for human behaviour. Failure in life is caused by denying or ignoring reality which may lead to a 'failure identity'. The basic concepts of this approach are as follows.

Identity: Reality therapy asserts that all people have a basic need for identity and a feeling of uniqueness from all others. This identity is involved with the role the person plays in life, and is linked with fulfilment which leads to a *success identity*. This need for a success identity is seen as a healthy force which drives people to achievement and fulfilment in life.

Involvement: Glasser maintains that people need to be involved with other people in a co-operative way so that we encourage and support one another.

Love and Worth: The basis for success today is seen to be a sense of being loved and being of worth to others. When people do not meet their needs for love and when they do not feel worthy through their achievements they suffer emotional and mental pain and move into a *failure identity*.

Responsibility: Responsibility is defined as the ability to fulfil one's own needs without depriving others of the ability to fulfil their needs. Thus responsible behaviour is typified by a person who achieves success and receives and gives love. Glasser believes that much mental illness is a demonstration of a failure identity, and that people choose a symptom to suffer from to reduce the pain of loneliness by seeking attention from other people. Glasser believes that when needs are successfully fulfilled by means of responsible behaviour then symptoms will disappear.

Reality: Glasser acknowledges that the behaviour of a psychologically ill person has validity to themselves, but in their lack of success he says that they have to deny the reality of the world around them.

Glasser views therapy as a form of training which helps the client to gain a realistic viewpoint and learn responsible behaviour and so achieve a successful identity. It is interesting to note the four qualities Glasser believes the counsellor needs to have to be a successful therapist.

1. A very responsible person, able to meet their own needs within the context of reality

2. Strength and integrity to resist clients' attempts to get the counsellor to collude with their belief and behaviour

3. Ability to accept and understand people who are isolated and in pain through failure to meet their own needs

4. Have the capacity to become emotionally involved with clients and so support them in their suffering

He then uses the seven principles of this approach to affect change in the client. These principles may be applied to individuals or within group sessions. Briefly they are as below, but for a more detailed description refer to Glasser's book *The Identity Society*.

PRINCIPLES OF REALITY THERAPY

Involvement: The therapist is warm and friendly, exhibiting acceptance and understanding, in order to break through the sense of failure of the client. The couple discuss a wide range of topics and avoid lengthy discussions of the client's problems.

Focus on current behaviour: Reality therapy focuses on changing the person's behaviour rather than their thinking processes or even their feelings. The emphasis is what they do, not how they feel whilst doing it, or even what they believe.

Evaluating behaviour: The client is encouraged to make value judgements about their behaviour and how good it is. The concept of alternative choices is stressed as people with emotional problems tend to see few, if any, alternatives to their behaviour pattern.

Planning responsible behaviour: The counsellor assists the client to understand and define their life goals, making sure that not too much is attempted too quickly since failure is counterproductive.

Commitment: The client makes a commitment (preferably written) to carry out responsible behaviour. This is important as it is seen that the key to feelings of self-worth is the ability to set and achieve goals.

No excuses: The assumption is made that a reasonable plan can always be achieved, so no excuses are accepted for failing to achieve.

No punishment: When the client succeeds they are praised, but no punishment is allowed as this reinforces the failure identity.

DISCUSSION OF REALITY THERAPY

This concept has much that will 'ring true' to the Christian. The basic principles are valid as far as they go, but the thing missing is the inner change of heart essential to a change in outward behaviour. A constant underlying problem in the church is that we fail to take our identity from God. Without this a 'success identity' must be superimposed from the outside in much the same way that pyramid sales companies hype up their sales personnel. The gaining of a success identity itself becomes a god which is always just out of reach. However, such people can be very 'good' people, genuinely aiming for self-fulfilment whilst helping other people. An identity in Christ allows for change from the inside-out.

RATIONAL-EMOTIVE THERAPY

Rational-emotive therapy emphasises that people create and sustain their emotional disturbances through irrational thinking and self-talk. This theory, founded by Albert Ellis, postulates that people have an innate tendency to irrationality. Therapy involves a mixture of cognitive, emotional and behavioural approaches. It aims to minimise clients' self-defeating outlooks which cause anxiety and thus help them acquire a more realistic and tolerant view of life. The basic concepts of this approach are:

Rationality: Ellis considered that humans have two basic goals - the first is to stay alive, and the second is to be happy. Rationality consists of ways of thinking which contribute to the attainment of both of these goals. Rationality is therefore defined as the use of mental reasoning in order to gain both short-term and long-term goals of survival and happiness.

Reason and emotion: Ellis proposed three basic ideas:-

1. Thinking and emotion are closely related.
2. Thinking and emotion act in a circular cause and effect relationship, so that one's thinking becomes one's emotions and vice-versa.
3. Both thinking and feeling take the form of *self-talk*, so the words that people keep saying to themselves are capable of generating and modifying emotions and thought patterns.

Appropriate emotions: Appropriate emotional responses are encouraged, so fear is natural in a dangerous situation to encourage vigilance. However, anxiety is seen as an inappropriate emotion as it is based on irrational thoughts.

Biological tendencies: Ellis believed that irrational behaviour is largely inbuilt in people, and most of us have great difficulty in modifying human irrationalities. This concept is not far removed from the idea of original sin, where the person has an inbuilt tendency to commit sin from birth.

BASIS OF R-E THERAPY

THE ABC FRAMEWORK
Ellis outlined a three stage process which acts as a framework for understanding how the irrational thoughts affect our emotions and consequent behaviour. **A** is the *activating event* - some event which affects us personally - such as being rejected in a relationship. **B** stands for the **beliefs and** *thoughts* about this event - which can be rational or irrational. Rational thoughts would be something like - "I am hurt and upset at being rejected, but it happens all the time, and the next time the relationship may develop." The irrational thought process would go - "I can't stand

being rejected, I am no good." **C** stands for the ***consequent behaviour and emotions*** which follows on from the rational or irrational thoughts. In the rational person the emotions would be of sadness and regret, but leading to a determination to try again and learn from this rejection to make better relationships in the future. The irrational person feels of no worth and is more likely to withdraw from future contacts so as not to get hurt again.

CHARACTERISTICS OF IRRATIONAL BELIEFS

Ellis listed the commonest irrational beliefs which people hold and which lead to most of their problems. The characteristics of these beliefs include demanding (both of self and others); over-generalisation - which takes a single event and assumes that all others will be similar; a tendency to perfectionism and therefore failure to be self-accepting, and a wrong attribution of motives to other people's actions.

CHANGING TO RATIONAL BELIEFS

This method of counselling relies heavily on changing irrational thoughts, and adds a **D** to the ABC framework which stands for ***debating and disputing*** these irrational beliefs in the client. The methods used will include teaching, exhortation, role modelling, role-playing situations, group discussion, homework and imagination techniques.

DISCUSSION OF R-E THERAPY

We see nothing in Ellis' observations of human nature regarding Rationality or Reason and Emotion that is contrary to what the Bible presents as basic human nature. However, the writer of the epistle to the Hebrews demonstrates that God intends us to develop higher goals than just staying alive and being happy. It is very obvious that the Bible would have no argument with the link between thinking and emotions. The idea of self-talk is all through the Bible. David says: 'Why are you downcast, O my soul? Why so disturbed within me? Put your hope in God,' and Paul seems to be aware that our thoughts feed our self-talk and therefore outlines a more effective mind focus in his letter to the Philippians. It is our experience that many of the observations of men like Ellis and Glasser are helpful as observations of human behaviour, and as such are morally neutral. However, values are always involved when strategies for change are developed, because change is always a value judgement.

TRANSACTIONAL ANALYSIS

Transactional analysis was originated by Eric Berne and is based on the understanding that humans start life from a basically satisfactory 'OK' position which is then lost through early childhood experiences. It describes three ego states of Parent, Adult and Child and seeks to analyse interchanges between people (called transactions), which demonstrate the ego state of the person and so stimulate them to develop into an integrated adult.

Transactional analysis (or TA for short) is one of the most popular modern models of counselling. It appeals especially to Christians, many of whom "integrate" it into their practice. Most people have heard of it's terms - Parent, Adult and Child; strokes; being OK or not-OK; recognising scripts and playing games.

Berne states that TA only makes two assumptions, or operates under only two principles: *Ego States* and *Transactions.*

Ego States: An ego state is defined as 'a system of feelings which motivates a related set of behaviour patterns'. The assumption therefore is that we all live in a particular ego state which consists of feelings and beliefs which have been acquired through life's experiences. The present ego state can be changed for a better one so that behaviour is modified to become more appropriate.

Through observations Berne identified three categories of ego states:

Parent: describes a set of feelings, attitudes and behaviour patterns which resemble those of the parent figure. There are two divisions of parent -

Prejudiced parent - exhibiting arbitrary values and prohibition
Nurturing parent - showing sympathy and support

Child: a set of feelings, attitudes and behaviour patterns which are relics of childhood. Again there are two divisions of the child ego -

Adapted child - dominated by parental influence, who either complies or withdraws
Natural child - who behaves independently with either creativity or rebellion

Adult: an autonomous set of feelings, attitudes and behaviour patterns which are correctly adapted to current reality.

Berne said that all of us have these three states throughout our lives, and they should be in harmony with one another, so each needs to be respected and therefore take its legitimate place. Ego states also have a historical description - we each have a life-plan or script which is formed by parental directives and the child's reactions and decisions.

Transactions: The second principle of TA concerns transactions which take place between people and can be assessed and verified. Berne called the unit of social intercourse a transaction. He said that these transactions take place between what he described as the three ego states (Parent, Adult and Child).

Berne described two sorts of people - winners and losers. And went on to describe the four life positions which stem from this.

I'M NOT OK - YOU'RE OK
The first position in childhood, often resulting from the trauma of birth and infancy. It is relieved by positive strokes from mother, but usually still persists well into childhood.

I'M NOT OK - YOU'RE NOT OK
If parents do not "stroke" the child this ingrained view persists throughout life. The person does not perceive any "strokes" from others as genuine.

I'M OK - YOU'RE NOT OK
An abused child turns in on its self and says that I'm OK so you go away. It is said that this state more often leads to criminality.

I'M OK - YOU'RE OK
State only reached by the adult as a conscious decision, when the person is able to move on from their inner feelings to develop rational thought processes.

THERAPY IN TA
The fourth position of hope - I'm OK and You're OK is the goal,

and is achieved by exposing the childhood predicament in the person. The goal of TA may be considered as enabling a person to have freedom of choice, the freedom to change at will, to change the responses to recurring and new stimuli. The ideal of human behaviour is to have the three capacities of *awareness* (I know how I feel and what is happening), *spontaneity* (I have the freedom to choose) and *intimacy* (I can love and be loved). Berne recognises that very few people reach this point of perfection, but it is something to strive towards. Therapy in TA mainly consists of *structural analysis* (a process of clarifying the ego states of the person) and *transactional analysis* (analysing interactions between the person and others - usually in a group setting).

DISCUSSION OF TA

There is much true observation of people in this model, but is it either true or helpful to believe that most of our problems arose in childhood? Certainly most of us have problems associated from trauma suffered during childhood, but how should this be dealt with? Sins we have committed, and sins of others against us which we have suffered do indeed need to be dealt with. While many Christian counsellors may use similar sorts of therapy, the basis of giving and receiving forgiveness is absent from the TA approach.

While an analysis of our interactions with others is always helpful, the final goal of TA to enable each person to have complete freedom of choice, and be able to change at will, is unrealistic without a heart change. We know the Holy Spirit to be the architect for a change of heart. As Christians we seek the same end, but by very different means. And it is good to remember that the end does not justify the means used to arrive at that end.

GROUP THERAPY APPROACHES IN COUNSELLING

All of the above methods of counselling are traditionally practised in the one-to-one situation. However, many counsellors also value working with groups of clients using drama, gestalt, and integrity group activities.

EGAN

Egan developed *contract-based encounter groups* in which group members are trained in specific ways of relating to others. He expected members of these groups to engage in the following core interactions:-

- self-disclosure, including expressing your feelings.
- listening to others and giving them support.
- confronting other people and responding to confrontation from others.

Group counsellors, rather more than individual counsellors, have to learn how to handle aggression within the groups. Often in the early stages of such groups there is considerable hostility and anger directed towards the counsellor and other members of the group. One of the main ways of dealing with this hostility is to encourage the client to use "I" sentences rather than "You" ones. It is much easier to handle someone who says "I feel angry when you do that" rather than "You make me angry".

GESTALT THERAPY

Fritz Perls developed Gestalt therapy which is usually conducted within groups. The aim of the therapy is to help clients make strong 'gestalts', or contact with their environment. People are encouraged to become more self-sufficient by increasing their ability to use the world for their own development rather than manipulating the environment by employing neurotic roles. Gestalt therapy concentrates on the 'here and now' by the use of drama and other techniques of getting people to expose and present their frustrations and resentments.

PSYCHOANALYTIC THEORIES OF COUNSELLING

Unlike the humanistic theories of counselling which emphasise a person's capacity to bring much of their behaviour under conscious control, the psychoanalytical model sees people as being more under the sway of their subconscious instincts. About 100 years ago Sigmund Freud started writing about his theories, and is usually referred to as the father of psychiatry. However it is worth pointing out that 100 years before Freud came on the scene, a German Christian named **Johann Heinroth** was practising and writing in the field of psychiatry. He first coined the phrase 'psychosomatic' to describe the relationship between psychological and physical illness. Heinroth believed in the tripartite nature of man, based on Paul's letter to the Romans, and divided the human person into three parts - conscience (the spirit), ego (the soul), and flesh (basic instincts and drives). One hundred years later Freud's division of personality into 'superego', 'ego' and 'id' may have been based on Heinroth's model. A further discussion on Henroth may be found in the book by Mieire and Minirth described in the end notes of chapter 5 of this book.

Both Heinroth and Freud described the struggle which occurs between the human conscience and the basic, selfish drives, but their solutions were quite different. Heinroth agreed with Paul in Romans that the soul was a victim of the flesh, and victory could only be achieved through the power of the Holy Spirit and the work of Christ on the cross. Freud taught that since the ego was an unconscious slave to the id, it was best to just accept this fact and so deaden the conscience, rather than accept guilt. Freud thought that guilt was one of the main causes of mental illness. Heinroth was not acknowledged by later psychiatrists because they held his spiritual and Christian views to be ridiculous, thus Freud is widely acknowledged as the father of psychiatry instead.

PSYCHOANALYTICAL APPROACHES TO COUNSELLING

For the sake of brevity we will outline the Freudian approach to psychoanalysis, although recognising that a large amount of thinking and developing have taken place over the last century by such people as Alfred Adler, Carl Jung and Erich Fromm. For a fuller understanding of the psychoanalytical approach we would recommend a general textbook on psychology.

The basic concepts of Freud's approach are to be found in his book *The Interpretation of Dreams*.

1. THE PLEASURE PRINCIPLE
This principle assumes that our minds attempt to keep excitation as low as possible, so we tend to seek for security and stability rather than change and uncertainty. Pleasure is experienced when we feel in control without any dangers looming. When we do seek excitement it must be on our terms, and we prefer to be in control.

2. THE INSTINCTS
Instinct represents a very basic biological demand upon the mind. Freud based his theory on the assumption that human instinct can be divided into two broad categories - the erotic

or life instinct, and the death or destructive instinct. The erotic or life instinct is one of self-preservation, continuation of the species and self-love. The energy of this instinct is called the libido. The death instinct may be viewed as a compulsion to destroy aggressively all that has been produced in self and others. These two instincts struggle within us, and no one is certain whether love will triumph over destruction.

3. CONSCIOUSNESS

Freud said that our thought lives occur on three levels - the *conscious*, the *preconscious* and the *unconscious*. The conscious mind is the part of us which perceives and experiences each moment. The unconscious part of the mind is divided into two - the unconscious mind proper which contains repressed memories and the pre-conscious which is a sort of gatekeeper between the two parts and is available to the conscious mind without any difficulty. It thus acts as a reservoir of memories which can be recalled when necessary.

4. STRUCTURE OF THE MIND

Freud divided the mind into three parts which he called the *id* (which is constantly striving to satisfy our instincts), the *ego* (which attempts to meet the demands of our instincts in the real world), and the *super-ego* (which represents parental and moral influence). The id was seen by Freud as "a chaos, a cauldron full of seething emotions, which knows no judgements of values: no good and evil, no morality." The ego acts as an intermediary between the id and the outside world and represents common sense and reason. The super-ego is that part of the ego which retains parental and cultural influences and acts as a moral brake on the ego and id. The id for example, would wish to indulge in a wide variety of activities which the super-ego would say are contradicted by society, so the ego looks around to see in what ways the id's desires can be fulfilled without contradicting the super-ego. This often produces a state of anxiety within the ego and the methods of compensation involve certain defence mechanisms.

5. ANXIETY

Freud saw anxiety as the reaction to danger and uncertainty in a person. He thought it resided in the ego. If the ego feels "weak" in relation to the threat then anxiety results, so the strength of the ego determines whether the anxiety experienced is appropriate or excessive. Thus realistic anxiety is a correct response to perceived dangers. Moral anxiety comes from an inner conflict between the ego and super-ego, and neurotic anxiety reflects a perceived weak ego which cannot cope with real or imaginary problems and dangers.

6. DEVELOPMENT OF THE PERSONALITY

A. INFANT

Clearly the early years of life are when we are most impressionable, and Freud believed that sexual life starts soon after birth. He believed that early sexual experiences leave deep traces in the personality. He used the term "infantile amnesia" to refer to the veil which is drawn over early sexual experiences. In infancy the child seeks pleasure mainly through experiences in his or her own body, but most of this is repressed and therefore not remembered later in life.

B. SEXUAL DEVELOPMENT

Freud said that there was an early pre-genital phase of sexuality up to the age of five which is followed by a period of latency until puberty when the genital phase begins. The pre-genital phase was said to comprise three stages - starting with the mouth (oral phase), followed by the anus (sadistic-anal phase) and finishing with the phallus (penis in male and clitoris in the female). The Oedipus phase is part of the phallic phase for both sexes. In the pre-genital phase the little boy identifies with his father, but in the phallic phase he sees his father as a threat and wishes to take his father's place in his mother's love. Freud said that the relative strengths of the masculine and feminine dispositions is what determines the outcome of whether the child identifies more with the father or the mother.

C. IDENTIFICATION

As we develop so we identify with those close to us, much of our belief and behaviour is influenced by what we now call 'role models'. The child needs to identify and so be moulded by the people around as he or she develops.

D. DEFENCE MECHANISMS

Defence mechanisms include regression, sublimation and projection. When the ego wishes to escape from difficult and unpleasant situations it may regress to an earlier stage and act in an infantile way. Sublimation involves a displacement of the instinctive impulses into acceptable alternative channels. Thus sexual desires may be sublimated into creative activities such as painting or poetry. If the unwanted feelings are not repressed or sublimated then they may be projected onto others by a process of criticism and condemning.

7. NEUROSES

Freud believed that neuroses are usually acquired during infancy as a result of the natural instincts being suppressed. Here the instincts have been repressed into the unconscious from where they exert an influence of frustration on the adult's behaviour. The aim of psychoanalysis is to strengthen the ego by lifting those early childhood repressions, bringing back the uncomfortable memories of childhood and altering the person's perception of themselves and their instincts.

PSYCHOANALYTIC THERAPY

Psychoanalytic therapy is a process of re-educating the ego through gaining insight and strengthening the process of making realistic decisions. The main tool for analysis is free-association in which the client tells the analyst everything that comes into their mind, even if it is disagreeable or appears meaningless. The analyst must interpret much of what is revealed by the client either openly or through dreams, and seeks to fill in the memory gaps of the client, so enabling the ego to cope better with repressed experiences. The counselling process is therefore only completed when all unconscious roots have been exposed and explained and so robbed of their power to influence the person.

FREE ASSOCIATION

The client must tell the analyst everything that comes into their mind, even if it is disagreeable or meaningless. The client is encouraged to put aside self-criticism and allow unconscious material to come into the consciousness.

RESISTANCE

There is an inbuilt resistance to allowing our repressed thoughts free rein, and free association or other methods of exploring the deeper levels of the person are resisted. The struggle to overcome resistance is the main work of psychoanalysis and cannot be hurried.

INTERPRETATIONS

Interpretation is the means whereby repressed and unconscious material is transformed into consciousness. The material for interpretation comes from free associations, slips of the tongue, dreams and analysis of relationships. Freud considered that the timing of interpretations was vital or else the client increased their resistance. During sleep the ego reduces its repression activity and unconscious material can take shape, so interpreting dreams can assist in the exploration of the unconscious mind.

TRANSFERENCE

Freud attached great importance to the nature of the relationship between client and therapist, with the analyst being in some ways the reincarnation of the important figures from the client's childhood. Thus the feelings and emotions which the person had towards these dominant influencers is transferred to the therapist. At first this may be positive, but as exploration proceeds and neuroses are uncovered the transference includes hostility, anger and jealousy.

BEHAVIOURAL THEORIES OF COUNSELLING

Behavioural theory is based on experimental attempts to understand the laws and principles by which human behaviour is first learned and then maintained. There are several schools of thought and experimentation within the behavioural therapies. Some of the main people associated with behavioural therapies are Ivan Pavlov, John Watson, Burrhus Skinner, Joseph Wolpe, Hans Eysenck and Albert Bandura.

Most behaviourists believe that mental and emotional illness are consequences of a learned response to the restrictions which other people place on the individual. These agencies of control will include parents, teachers and religious institutions. The therapist largely acts to affirm the client and make them feel less 'wrong or sinful' so that repressed behaviour can come to the surface. The therapist develops a degree of control over the client and reinforces those beliefs and actions which the therapist believes will lead to a more appropriate form of behaviour. A more detailed description of behavioural psychology can be obtained by standard secular counselling textbooks such as that by Nelson-Jones mentioned earlier.

WATSON'S CONDITIONED BEHAVIOURISM

John Watson (1878 - 1958) is viewed as the founder of behaviourism, which concentrates on the behaviour of the person as the clue to both understanding and producing change in people's personalities. Watson reckoned that a person can only change if they first un learn harmful habits and then re-learn good ones. He emphasised the importance of training and habit forming, that is good behaviours will eventually lead to good thoughts and emotions. Watson defined personality as the sum of activities that can be discovered by observation of behaviour over a long period of time, thus personality is the end product of our habit patterns. He suggested five ways of obtaining an accurate estimate of personality:

1. education chart;
2. achievement chart;
3. spare time and recreation record;
4. emotional make-up under the situations of daily living;
5. psychological tests.

Thus personality problems are really disturbances of behaviour and habit conflicts which need to be cured by first de-conditioning and then reconditioning.

SKINNER'S OPERANT BEHAVIOURISM

Burrhus Skinner developed many of his theories after extensive studies on pigeons and rats. Whilst a response to a stimulus cannot be predicted, there is an increased probability that future reactions will be similar if the same stimulus is applied. The term 'operant' emphasises the fact that behaviour operates on the environment to generate consequences. Skinner stressed the role played by the environment in both causing and maintaining behaviour, and so his descriptions contained three elements:-

1. the occasion in which a response occurs;
2. the response itself;
3. the reinforcing consequences.

The probability of a response is increased after either negative or positive reinforcements are introduced. One major implication of his approach is in people with serious mental health problems which he suggested are extreme consequences of the person's behaviour. Psychotherapy is therefore aimed at correcting the undesirable effects of either excessive or inadequate control over the individual's behaviour patterns.

WOLPE'S RECIPROCAL INHIBITION

Wolpe began to experiment with cats and developed a method based on reciprocal inhibition in order to de-condition neurotic responses. He applied this method to people with neuroses. Wolpe noticed that old habits are often overcome by developing new habits in the same situation, so the term reciprocal inhibition implies that developing an alternate response may replace a harmful habit in a given situation. Wolpe defined neurotic behaviour as any persistent habit or harmful behaviour acquired by a person, usually involving a degree of anxiety. He mainly used relaxation and self-assertive techniques to overcome these neuroses.

Other proponents of behavioural therapy have included Albert Bandura and Hans Eysenck, who was largely responsible for its acceptance with the general public.

NEURO-LINGUISTIC PROGRAMMING

In the 1970's John Grinder and Richard Bandler developed a new understanding of human behaviour, much of which is based on previous models of behavioural change. They called it Neuro-Linguistic Programming (NLP) as it focuses on the verbal and non-verbal activities (linguistics) which pass along our neural pathways to produce thinking patterns and behaviours which make up our experience of life. Programming is the way this content is directed, sequenced and connected by each one of us.

They discussed the "internal reality maps" which make up our "world view" and through which we make sense, observe and react to the world of experience. The aim of the programming is to gain understanding of both your own map and that of other people to produce success in life and relationships.

NLP distinguishes between the outer and the inner sensory experience. The outer senses include the well known seeing, hearing, touching, smelling etc. The inner senses include our thoughts, feelings, ideas and responses. In other words they postulated that thinking itself is a sensory event as thoughts are made up of inner pictures, remembered smells and feelings as well as sounds (or words).

NLP seeks to understand the structure of human experience and consists of a set of models and methods which explore how we create and maintain successful decision making, motivation and learning. Much of the methodology used is empirical (rather than research based), and much relies on a re-working of methods used in other counselling approaches.

At the heart there is much common-sense in this approach, although many practitioners combine it with hypnosis and other similar methods of producing behavioural changes in the person's beliefs and actions. Whilst it is obviously vital that we understand better both ourselves and those we relate to, the evidence that these programming techniques are both successful and without harm is still not available. This is becoming a growth area in counselling but in our view should be treated with caution as the full implications of the theoretical and experiential basis have not been evaluated.

CONCLUSIONS

It is worth reminding ourselves that all of the secular approaches described above are based on a specific theoretical view of mankind. There is much good observation and common sense in many approaches, but most, if not all, are **not based** on the Christian understanding of mankind, although many words and concepts may appear to be familiar to us. Those desiring to integrate elements of these theories and approaches into their counselling must very cautiously consider how consistent they are with the aims and objectives of Christianity. This consideration is not limited to whether or not the counsellor is encouraging or condoning things like abortion, divorce or cohabitation. The question is also: *'Is this procedure teaching or reinforcing un-biblical values or habits in the client?'* Secular counselling models are not neutral frames which can be 'baptised' to support a Christian canvas any more than one could 'sanctify' the Humanist Manifesto by adding a couple of Bible texts. One may find secular elements that can be imported into a Christian model, but one can't expect a secular model to effectively support and convey Christianity. A very useful book which critiques the various approaches to counselling, both secular and Christian is *Roots and Shoots* by Roger Hurding.

REFERENCES FOR SECULAR COUNSELLING

The Theory and Practice of Counselling, Richard Nelson-Jones, published by Holt, Rinehart and Winston, London 1982
Humanist Manifesto II, published in 1973
Client-centred therapy, Carl Rogers, published by Houghton Mifflin, Boston 1951
The Identity Society, William Glasser (revised edition), published by Harper and Row, New York 1975
Humanistic Psychology. The Rational-emotive approach, A Ellis, published by Julain Press, New York 1973
Transactional Analysis in Psychotherapy, Eric Berne, published by Grove Press, New York 1961
New introductory lectures on psychoanalysis, S. Freud, 1973, published by Penguin books, UK
The skilled helper, Gerard Egan, published by Brooks/Cole, Belmont California, USA 1982
Gestalt Therapy, Perls, F., Hefferline, R.F. & Goodman, P, published by Souvenir Press, London 1951
Roots and Shoots, Roger Hurding, published by Hodder and Stoughton, London 1985.

APPENDIX B

The following spiritual purity and occult 'inventory' is one of several which have circulated within the church at large for years. With regard to copyright we have no notion of its origin and assume it to be totally anonymous, ours was a photocopy of a photocopy. Many Christians attempting to minister in cases where the occult is suspected to be a factor have found such lists helpful. You may not agree that all items listed are of any consequence but the list is a starting point to develop your own.

SPIRITUAL PURITY AND THE OCCULT

Most of us have not been well educated in the ways Satan can infect us spiritually. Read Deut. 18:9-14 - well known in Christ's time. See 2 Thess. 2:9, Rev. 16:14, Acts 13, Luke 11:19-20. Eph. 6:12. The 'abominations' do weaken faith and cause spiritual darkness when we need spiritual enlightenment.

Use this list to allow the Holy Spirit to speak to you as you test yourself with these questions and then seek for cleansing through ministry by Spirit-filled elders with confession, renouncing, forgiveness being pronounced and, if necessary, deliverance and healing.

Are you aware that either of your parents, or any grandparent, was involved in spiritualism or any occult practices?

Are you aware that any other relative or person that you have had close contact with at any time was similarly involved?

Have you ever been aware of 'voices' speaking to you in your mind? (Not to be confused with the Holy Spirit's gentle prompting).

Do you feel that you are 'psychic' and that you are

sometimes made aware of future events?

Have you ever delved into:

• reincarnation pagan religions claiming them to be good instead of acknowledging Christ as the only way to God?

• Metaphysics - E.S.P.

• Mind science

• Yoga (exercises based on Hindu gods), other cults, transcendental meditation, spiritualism or magic?

Have you ever taken horoscopes even remotely seriously?

Have you attended a seance?

Have you been to a medium, fortune teller, palm reader?

Have you played with a Ouija board or tarot cards, for guidance or even just for fun?

Have you been involved in divining for water?

Have you ever submitted yourself to hypnosis, which is not bringing your mind subject to Christ alone?

Have you sought the help of any occult healer?

Have you ever taken mind expanding drugs, such as LSD or 'pot' or marijuana?

Have you practised superstitions or given lip service to them?

Have you deliberately used pornography, engaged in any sexual relations outside marriage?

Using pornography and all forms of sexual sins are a door to occult forces.

Have you committed yourself to a secret society, spiritual or semi-spiritual organisation that omits Jesus?

Have you lived in a primitive country where witchcraft or spirits might have been directed against you, including spells?

Have you engaged in or had involvement in any of the practices below:

Mind control. Mental telepathy. Clairvoyance. Casting spells. Using a divining rod or pendulum - even a wedding ring - swinging it to predict the sex of an unborn child? Table-tipping, levitation, astral travel and automatic writing.

PLEASE NOTE: We feel it is important to stress that this exercise needs to be led by the Holy Spirit with wise elders or clergy and not with people intent on a witch-hunt, who interpret all problems as demonic.

APPENDIX C

WE OFFER THE FOLLOWING counselling contract as a sample of the type of thing counsellors and counselling groups should be considering. This is an actual document which was made available to us by a well established Christian counselling service with an excellent reputation among both their counselling colleagues and the community. It is presented exactly as it appears with the exception that it covers only one side of an A4 sheet in real life. As you can see they don't refer to it as a contract and it may not be exactly suited to your needs, but it is a starting point.

The Manna House Counselling Service

TERMS of COUNSELLING

We believe that it is important to ensure that the counselling we offer is as helpful and effective as possible. We have, therefore, compiled these "Terms of Counselling" in order to help reduce the possibility of any misunderstanding between ourselves and our clients. We use the term "client" to refer to those who come to us for help.

1. Initially, we offer up to four sessions (unless a smaller number seem necessary) after which the effectiveness of the counselling process will be evaluated by your counsellor(s) and their supervisor. An extension of the period of counselling may then be agreed but will be subject to regular reviews with the counsellor(s) and their supervisor. If it is thought to be in the client's best interest, or in the case of illness, another member of the team may be introduced.

2. The client has the right at any time to terminate the counselling. The Manna House Counselling Service asks that, in such circumstances, as much notice as possible should be given.

3. The Manna House Counselling Service may terminate counselling if, after discussion with the client, it is felt that further counselling would be either inappropriate or would not be beneficial to the client.

4. The Manna House Counselling Service receives many more requests for help than can be met, therefore, if a client fails to keep appointments without reasonable notice, it may be necessary to terminate counselling and offer the time to another client. Appointments will normally be for one hour, so punctuality is important.

5. The Manna House Counselling Service cannot accept responsibility for the client's response to counselling and the client acknowledges that any advice or assistance given in the course of counselling does not create any legal liability on the part of the Manna House Counselling Service.

6. Sometimes a counsellor will suggest certain tasks for a client to work on between sessions; this is intended to reinforce the effectiveness of the counselling. Such "assignments" should be agreed between counsellor and client and should be seen as important and therefore not treated lightly.

7. Confidentiality is a key element in our practice but due consideration should be given before disclosing anything of a criminal nature as the Manna House does have certain legal obligations. As standard professional procedure, summary notes will be made and will be kept in a locked cabinet.

8. The Manna House Counselling Service asks that, as evidence of your understanding and acceptance of these terms, you sign one copy of these "terms" and hand it to your counsellor at the commencement of counselling.

9. The Manna House Counselling Service provides help free of

charge but donations are always very welcome.

....

I agree to the terms set out on this sheet and will co-operate, to the best of my ability, with my Counsellor.

Signed :- .... Client

Signed :- .... For Manna House Counselling
                            Service.
 Date :- ....

MHCS TofC Page 1.(Apr '95)

END OF SAMPLE CONTRACT

A HUMBLE CONFIDENCE *A Christian Perspective on Self-image* by Dave Ames

Have you ever been to a Christian conference where feelings of inferiority where presented as humility and therefore a sign of godliness? Have you ever read a Christian book that implied that loving ones self (as in love your neighbour as your self) meant being pleased with all that we are? This is a subject where the boundaries between misguided fundamentalism and secular humanism are not well charted. It is one ridge that we must tread with the skill of a mountain goat, because in places it is very narrow with disastrous pitfalls on both sides.

SELWYN HUGHES READ *A HUMBLE CONFIDENCE* AND SAID:

When I first perused it I had the image of a doctor walking into a stuffy and closed-up room of one of his patients and throwing open the windows to let in a stream of much needed fresh air. The 'fresh air' in this case is the pure oxygen of the Scriptures.

A Humble Confidence addresses the secular misconceptions most frequently imported into the Church, provides answers to the most common questions and suggests some highly effective ways to earth Christian truth into this familiar problem.

A HUMBLE CONFIDENCE addresses the following questions and many more.

To what extent is our self-image pre-programmed by our childhood experiences, and just how indelible is such early childhood programming?

What is the effect of our current successes or failures?

Can we actually survive without some 'positive strokes'?

Is it possible to love others if we don't love ourselves?

Is self-love biblical?

Should we view ourselves as worms?

How is it possible to feel good about ourselves even when actual performance figures seem to prove we are inferior?

Is it possible even though we know we are dealing with a sin problem?

How do we remove barriers that prevent us developing a healthy self-image?

This is not a book about what is wrong with current self-esteem theories - It does address these, but it is a book providing 'handholds' on a very real problem. It is a positive, practical and much needed book! Like *Looking Up The Aisle?*, it is available at Christian book shops at £4.50.

THE BOOK THAT LAUNCHED
A THOUSAND MARRIAGES

(A FEW TIMES OVER)

Marriage counselling consists largely of listening to couples tell of their problems and quietly identifying principles that are being violated. In other words we need to know the problems and why they have arisen in order to help the couple. However, pre-marriage is entirely different because we are dealing with a couple who in all probability won't be able to spot even the slightest hint of a problem on the horizon. Some young couples have felt it was judgmental to even suggest that they might have problems some day. This leaves the counsellor with the responsibility of stimulating their thinking in various decision areas to prove to them that they don't necessarily agree on everything and alerting them to the necessity of developing ways of handling their varying opinion.

The heart of marriage preparation is helping couples explore their expectations, negotiate their differences and develop their realistic expectations into goals and objectives that reflect Christian values. *LOOKING UP THE AISLE?* provides a biblical context for couples to examine their expectations. Each partner reads the agreed chapter and answers the questions at the end of the chapter. The couple then exchange workbooks and read how the other answered the question. They are then encouraged to dialogue over any differences in order to determine what their stand, as a couple, will be on that particular issue. The product of these discussions becomes 'benchmarks' for future decisions.

LOOKING UP THE AISLE? has a supplement for those with previous marriage experience as they have additional issues to discuss. The necessity of this supplement is not limited to divorcees. Those who have been widowed have just as many problems as those who have experienced marriage failure. Supplements are £1 each directly from Mission to Marriage.

LOOKING UP THE AISLE? wasn't meant to be used on its own, although it certainly can be if necessary. It was meant to be used in conjunction with another couple who are committed Christians and have a sound marriage. The engaged couple would complete a chapter per week and meet fortnightly with the married couple to discuss their progress and findings. The married couple would use questions to explore whether the engaged couple were actually coming to grips with the material and the issues raised. Mission to Marriage produces a kit to equip the married couple for this task. It contains 200 minutes of lectures on cassette tapes of the authors training couples to enter into this task. There is also two sets of lecture notes that are, in actuality, a leaders guide as each page covers a chapter in the workbook. The kit also contains a copy of *LOOKING UP THE AISLE?* and the supplement for those with previous marriage experience and sells for only £12 at this point in time. As with the supplements, to keep the price low means it is not a commercially viable product that can be sold through book shops and it is only available from Mission to Marriage direct.